We Walk on Water

Cara Cobb

La Maison Publishing, Inc.

Maison

Vero Beach, Florida
The Hibiscus City
www.lamaisonpublishing.com

This book is dedicated to those I love in the Move and out of the Move. These stories thread through your lives and weave into my heart forever.

To my three children, their spouses and my six grandchildren: I leave you this my book. It is who I am. I am thinking there will be more books, we shall see.

To my closet friend and sister: You have overflowed my cup.

To Sammy: The best puppy in the whole wide world.

To Barb T.: You are the only one who understands why I cannot remember the name of an old boyfriend.

My dearest Tracy. I can only say "Thank you." You not only gave me space, you built me space. Honey, we're the big door prize.

Prologue

"You just need to go home and stroke your husband's penis." These were words of counsel from a Move minister to whom I had opened my heart concerning my husband's infatuation with a woman in our "fellowship." As a wife, I was to stay in my rightful place as a "helpmate" to my man. Period. After thirty-nine years of marriage, it was not my place to question his marital faithfulness, despite.

"The Move" is the media tag given a worldwide religious organization founded and led by two men. There were/are cells in Europe, Asia, Africa, South America, Central America, Canada, Australia and the U.S. Communities, of which few remain, were established in the frozen wildernesses of Alaska and Canada and in the raw jungles of Peru and Colombia. Each community or "city group" is autonomous with its own registered church name and its own governing faction of appointed elders. All Move groups are tied together by a fraternity of "traveling ministry" and "father ministry" who travel from group to group, preaching a consistent thread, settling community issues and appointing local elders. These men (there were/are wives and female preachers with minimal input included in this group) ascended from the original core of the two men. Move conventions conducted at Bowen's Mill, Georgia, and other locales keep local congregations united with visiting members from far places.

For writing ease, I will eliminate the quotation marks from "the Move."

I find little disparity between the definitions of a "cult" and a "sect." For clarity and consistency, I will define the Move as a cult. I used to scoff when the term was loosely applied to our community in Wilcox County, Georgia. Jim Jones, the Brethren, Mormonism, Davidian Branch---these were cults, not us. The Move is indeed a cult, founded around the teachings of two men who claimed to have heard personally from God.

Carrell (Buddy) Cobb was one of those men. I was his favorite daughter-in-law, married to his only son. As a married couple and then as a family of five, we lived intimately with Buddy and Dottie Cobb for thirty-one years, eight of which were spent sharing a home with them.

Sam Fife was the other man. I met Sam and his wife, Lee, when I was a newlywed eighteen-year-old in Hollywood, Florida. Sam and Lee were often guests in the Cobb home, both in Florida and, later, in Georgia. I knew Sam jogged barefoot and put salt on his watermelon. Sam told me I would be a great demon chaser, I believed him. Lee was my champion, but she died too soon to help.

I came into the Move in 1970 in Hollywood, Florida. Eight years later, our family moved to New Covenant Fellowship located near Fitzgerald, Georgia. We built the community with others who had left jobs, families, and financial security in the attempt to be holy, harmless, undefiled, and separate from the World. We lived and breathed Biblical principles as taught by the ministry of the "Move." We educated our own children, we grew gardens and raised livestock, we shared meals, and we birthed our babies at home. We prepared ourselves to rule and reign with Christ at the end of the Great Tribulation. Some in town said that we walked on water.

My tales may not reflect common opinion, other's experiences, general thought, Move mentality, or time sequence. I lived the life from 1970-2009. Though names, places, and circumstances may be changed, these are my tales.

Cara S. Cobb
October 14, 2018

We Walk on Water

For my daughter's high school graduation announcements, my husband and she drove his pick-up to the blue-spring, which flowed clear, cold water into the Ocmulgee River. She stood in the frigid knee-high water atop an upside-down five-gallon bucket. He took the photo with the intention of making it seem as if she were walking on water.

Mr. Dorsey, president of Dorsey Bank, received one of the announcements and promptly had it framed and mounted on his office wall. He proudly showed it off with the comment, "See that photo? Those people out there walk on water!"

A budding, talented artist, Julia Martinez, created my cover illustration from that photo. She chose to add quiet symbolism to my story through the flowers adorning the figure's head:

Bittersweet: Truth

White Carnation: Purity, Innocence

Heather: Protection, Solitude, Admiration

Yellow Lily: Positives, Happiness;
"Walking on Air"

Daisy: Innocence, Loyalty, Purity

Grass: Submission and Community

1985

In the early 1960's, a Southern guitar player from New Orleans left his band, The Southern Playboys, to answer a "call of God." Sam Fife pounded neighborhood doors proclaiming the impending end of days and the necessity of a God-fearing life. He was built like a lightweight fighter; his steely grey eyes could pierce through any veiled conscience. Using his gifted charisma, Sam preached, he laid hands on the sick and commanded demons to flee. He delivered an urgent message that seemed obviously necessary for the times:

Babylon is falling; come out of Babylon and flee to the wilderness. The Tribulation is coming and only through the blood of Jesus Christ can any be spared. We who are thus called will be the corporate Man-child, born of God to rule and reign in God's coming new world. Leave all, forsake all, and follow Him.

Meanwhile, my father-in-law, Buddy Cobb, a commercial airline pilot, was born-again during a hotel-room confrontation with God. Recanting his frivolous lifestyle, he returned home to eagerly share his newfound faith and convictions with his family.

In 1965, my husband and his older sister were graduating from high school, the younger sister was a middle schooler in the throes of early adolescence. The announcement of their dad's spiritual rebirth fell on incredulous ears as they calculated the loss of friends, parties, extracurricular activities, and social freedoms.

The older daughter swept away to college, married and became a teacher in Miami-Dade schools. Although, she also taught in the Hollywood's Move school, she and her family never moved into community, choosing to relocate in North Carolina where she continued her public-school teaching career.

The son escaped via his 1964 yellow Mustang convertible using it to drive to a job in Key West, until he was drafted and shipped-out to Berlin. Which is where we met when I was a lifeguard at the base swimming pool.

The younger daughter was trapped in a new world of long skirts, no dates, the end of "pagan" music, limited friendships, and hours of church services and Bible studies. She married young, entered the Move and later left to enjoy days with her life-long partner and husband.

Buddy and his wife, Dottie, had been active members of a Methodist Church. Buddy had been the regular Sunday school teacher. During his spiritual awakening, he claimed the Baptism of the Holy Spirit whose presence was confirmed by the gift of glossolalia, or "speaking in tongues." Having shared his heavenly experience with his Sunday class, he was subsequently ousted from the Methodist church. With a group of faithful who followed him out of the church, Buddy began leading Bible study meetings in his Hollywood Hills home and performing water baptisms in the cool waters of his backyard pool.

Soon after in what is called "God's perfect timing," Buddy encountered Sam Fife slamming out Jesus music with three chords on his acoustic guitar, his guttural Southern twang bellowing: "Awake, Zion, Awake!"

Buddy was smitten with the impassioned, wiry figure, finding his own genteel, yet commanding disposition bonding with Sam's vibrant personality. Buddy and Sam often joked that they had absolutely nothing in common other than their shared "vision" for the church. They maintained a tight spiritual connection until Sam's death in 1979, when he crashed his plane into a Guatemalan mountainside.

I first encountered Sam Fife snoozing in the family room of my in-law's home as, bikini-clad, I slid open the heavy glass door leading to the pool deck. From the depths of the Lazy Boy, he rasped "Daughter of Zion, when are you ever going to put on some clothes?" It was the first time I felt naked in a two-piece.

Buddy told me, "Accepting Jesus into your life is like trading in your old jalopy of a car for a brand-new Cadillac." Sure, I wanted a Cadillac life, but I was not looking for religion and my new husband stayed way-far-away from his father's church.

The spiritual journey of my youth had taken me into mind control, telepathy and astral travel. I performed handwriting analysis for friends, family and my dad's office staff. I skidded a planchette around a Ouija board hoping it was not my fingers doing the walking. I was convinced I could soar below my bedroom ceiling, and dart invisibly into my big brother's room to hover inches from his head. I received messages from avoiceinsidemyhead.

So, when Buddy explained the indwelling Presence of an all-powerful, ever present, loving, caring spirit God, I knew I had to meet Him. Following Buddy's direction, I burned all my witchcraft books, handwriting analysis books, Carlos Castaneda books and Ouija board. I placed my collection of worldly music, original cover Beatle albums, Rolling Stones and Jefferson Airplane on the curb for the astounded garbage truck driver.

After my "house was swept," I followed Buddy into the den where others were seated on chairs arranged in a circle. He explained to them that I was wanting "The Baptism of the Holy Spirit." Amid hushed choruses of "Amen's" and "Praise the Lord's," they stood around me placing their hands on my back, shoulders, head, arms; Buddy placed his warm hand on my forehead. As their volume rose with their enthusiasm, incomprehensible language came from their mouths, Buddy's hand pushed harder. "In the name of Jesus! Give her your Spirit now, Lord! Cara, just open your mouth and let the words flow out."

Sam and Lee Fife

Miss Lee and Me

My husband's close friend, Tomas, was an extremely good-looking, forever-youthful man. In 1972, Tomas was living with his mother in her two-bedroom duplex apartment a few blocks from the Hollywood Fashion Square. His charming, Hungarian mother, Aliz, had supported their way beginning as a Vegas girl and settling as head barmaid at Holiday Inn. A rich boyfriend or two helped supplement their modest livelihood.

Aliz rented us the opposite half of their duplex and, being closer to our two friends, we became one happy family. Tomas had a series of visiting girlfriends; gorgeous, olive skinned, longhaired Jewish princesses; I befriended all of them. Raven-haired Linda was shapely, healthily endowed, highly intelligent and drove a sassy VW Karmen Ghia convertible. She and her younger sister lived with their mom, a successful, real-estate attorney, on a four-lane Hollywood avenue banked by cookie-cutter ranch-style homes, each with its postage stamp front yard inclining into the busy street.

Linda loved her cat, a fat, often pregnant, calico female. I loved my dog, an amiable Afghan hound named Hussan.

Hussan accompanied me everywhere, being often mistaken for a sexy blonde woman riding in my car.

Ever adventurous, Linda had become actively involved in a Hollywood witches' coven.

The head warlock was a powerful, prominent South Florida lawyer. A massive "magical" stone occupied the front corner of his property. Town gossip claimed that undecipherable carvings on the stone revolved in a concentric pattern. One dark, night, a bold prankster swiped the stone to quickly return it following a front-page newspaper ad's proclaiming the stone's demonic powers.

Linda had been ceremoniously chosen to be the October 31 Sabbath's virgin sacrifice for the coven. The role of virgin sacrifice included lying naked on a flat table while each of the coven priests engaged in intercourse with her. Linda was not a virgin and she was not interested in having sex with old Satanic priests, so she declined the invitation. The coven retaliated by flooding Linda's sleep with horrific nightmares followed by bleeding, beheaded small animals left ceremoniously on her mother's front porch. Linda got scared. I had shared my recent spiritual experience with her and encouraged her to come to the Move church to seek protection from the evil attacking her. She responded most unenthusiastically.

Linda and I shared a part-time, well-paying job. Qualified by our young, beachie looks, we spent our working hours as a greeter of a luxurious Hollywood Beach condo model to warmly welcome wealthy, prospective buyers. I took Hussan and positioned him next to the desk as elegant eye candy with doggie appeal.

Early one fall morning, following routine, I drove the two miles to Linda's home to retrieve the condo key for my shift; Hussan rode passenger in my snazzy VW Fastback. I parked on the edge of the sidewalk in front of her house, got out of the car and walked around to let the dog out, leaving his door hanging open for breeze. With Hussan's leash securely wrapped around my hand, I approached her front door and announced our arrival with the booming brass doorknocker. Wrapped in a bath towel, her long, wet hair streaming, Linda swung open the door to slip me the key poised in her fingers. Suddenly — Her normally friendly, fat feline lunged from behind her, claws extended, to alight on top of my head. I screamed, turned and fell off the porch into the thick grass, swiping frantically at the howling banshee on my head. Relinquishing the leash, I commanded Hussan to GET INTO THE CAR!

The maddened cat was scraping her claws repeatedly around my torso while trying to sink her incisors through my thick hair. With my face buried in the dense lawn, I wrapped my arms protectively around my head. My thoughts moved to the traffic threat and the safety of my dog; a slight turn of my head assured the sight of Hussan perched anxiously on the front seat. The cat enveloped me with her four legs and gouged her teeth repeatedly through my clothing.

I crawled to my car and finally managed somehow, to rake off the cat. Slamming the dog's door, I stumbled to the driver's side and slid gratefully in. I glanced back to the porch to see Linda standing motionless; wrapped in her towel; transfixed in the open doorway; the key dangling from her fingers.

I drove the few blocks to my in-law's home, and plunged through the front door, sobbing hysterically. I was incoherent, the back of my blouse was shredded revealing a roadway of bleeding claw tracks and open puncture wounds. My mother-in-law led me into the shower, then peeled my blood-soaked top from my torn back as I blurted out the horrifying encounter. She counted 23 back bites and numerous claw marks that traced from my spine to under my breasts. She settled Hussan, then drove me to the doctor.

Dr. M. wanted the cat quarantined. It never happened. I did not file a police report and Linda ignored the doctor's order. Linda's mother kept a low profile in the situation, hoping it would go away.

That evening, I attended a scheduled church meeting at the storefront church on Dixie Highway in Hollywood. At the end of service, there was a customary prayer time and Dottie asked if I wanted healing for my painful, swollen wounds. I said, "No. I want to pray for the soul of my friend, Linda." I walked past the rows of grey metal folding chairs to the wooden pulpit where the congregation laid their hands on me and prayed in tongues for my friend, Linda.

By the next morning, the only physical evidence of the vicious feline attack was thin white claw scars ribboning across my back and around to my chest. All the bite wounds were healed.

I have not since seen or heard from my friend, "Cat Linda."

Caesar Salad from Caesar's Palace in Las Vegas
Shared with me by Aliz, who died too young

Torn, crispy Romaine lettuce, tossed with a coddled egg; flavored with one pressed garlic clove; dripped with pure olive oil and freshly squeezed lemon juice; dusted generously with freshly grated Parmesan cheese; sprinkled with coarsely ground black pepper and sea salt and draped in a can of anchovies.

As leftovers, Caesar Salad becomes a delightfully tasty mess of flavors, soaked croutons and soggy Romaine.

By 1972, The Move had morphed into a wide network with "city groups" evolving in

New York, Ohio, Florida, Pennsylvania, Maine, Georgia, DC, Minnesota, Oklahoma, Texas, California, Mexico, South America and Canada. The fellowship in Hollywood, Florida, grew to nearly 100 members.

Hollywood opened the first Move school to free our children from the influences of public education and be trained up "in the fear and admonition of the Lord." We opened the school with a handful of pupils and two certified teachers who left education careers to qualify us as a legit private Christian school. It was a scary thing for parents and an awesome responsibility for the teachers. On my water-safety instructor certification and God's recommendation, I was asked to teach.

It was decided that we, the teachers, would travel daily from house to house, teaching in each home. As an itinerant teacher I was assigned three first graders living in three separate homes. Despite their diverse backgrounds, the families were attempting to meld their beliefs of religion, child raising and education into agreement with Move "order."

Sam Fife taught that children, as "little beasts" were born with a predisposition for evil. (Gen. 8:21 "The LORD smelled the pleasing aroma and said in his heart: 'Never again will I curse the ground because of humans, even though every inclination of the human heart is evil from childhood. '") The directive was that a child must obey on the first command, or an immediate sound spanking followed. The parents were frustrated and frequently misconstrued the mandate to mean beating a child into "choosing good rather than evil." I watched, shuddering inside, as one father beat his three-year-old daughter with a belt until she confessed to a lie rather than repeat what was truth.

Sam and Buddy had gained a tight core of disenchanted denominational preachers who formed an elite group of ministries, predominately male, who called themselves "Father Ministry." Their sermons unequivocally correlated and confirmed "the Truth" as interpreted by them. In the turbulent 1970's, their promises of peaceful co-existence and God's blessings through corporate life in the wilderness attracted free-thinking college students, disillusioned professionals and lonely single women. As the call to leave Babylon snowballed into mass exoduses of various "city groups" to desolate and sequestered destinations, communal farms were established in rough wilderness areas of Alaska, drug cartel-controlled jungles of Central and South America and the deep dark areas of Africa. Well-educated, multi-talented, youthful American Caucasians lived primitively and intimately with natives of all skin colors; actively living a life of self-sacrifice without modern conveniences or adequate health care; believing that they were fulfilling the "Perfect Will of God."

Watching the migration of Move groups as they "fled to the wilderness," the Hollywood congregation began preparing for their own exodus. Buddy and Sam had located two pieces of available property in the piney woods of rural Georgia. I accompanied them on a first visit to the properties, flying from Perry Airport to the Fitzgerald Municipal Airport in Fitzgerald, Georgia.

After lunch at a restaurant, which displayed a "Whites Only" sign over their water-fountain, we headed to a large property twelve miles north of Fitzgerald on Highway 129, which was owned by a failing real estate corporation.

A spot high on a sandy ridge in Ben Hill County had been the former home of a post-WWII CCC camp which had housed workers building the highway network connecting small town America to urban areas. Adjoining the ridge was an abandoned restaurant, motel, gas station, bowling alley and swimming pool. This had once been a popular recreational center linked to Fitzgerald by a short train track during the 1950's and '60's. House Creek, a tributary off the Ocmulgee River, crosses under Highway 129 hiding remnants of Bowen's Mill, a corn-grinding water-wheel built in 1836, on its southern bank. The property extended into woods on the west side of the highway, completing nearly 650 acres of available land.

With direction from Sam and Buddy, the property was purchased and became Bowen's Mill Christian Center, Inc. and the site of our school, the convention center and a deliverance farm.

A "deliverance farm" is a Move community established to house and care for those with physical, mental or emotional disabilities. The initial such community, located in Homestead, Florida, was founded on the premise that healing could be accomplished through the deliverance of demonic presence and maintained by 24/7 behavioral monitoring. The residents were given meals, housing, supervision, daily tasks and hours of Bible indoctrination. The work had grown to necessitate their first move from Homestead to Sapa, Mississippi, where the population had enlarged to nearly 200 occupants, both "deliver'ers" and "deliver-ees." (Although, it was claimed that all were there for deliverance.) Following legal entanglements, the sheriff of Webster County urged the community's leaders to relocate to another state. In the winter of 1977, the Sapa Farm caravanned their residents, animals and farm equipment to Bowen's Mill, settling into aluminum mobile homes on the edge of Highway 129 in Ben Hill County and becoming The Ridge.

Two miles north of Bowen's Mill, in Wilcox County, and hardly visible from the highway was a one-hundred forty acres' hunting lodge (owned by the same realty corporation). Originally the residence of Confederate Captain Fuller, the white, two-story

Plantation Style home passed through generations to evolve into a weekend retreat for prospective land-buyers and corporate real estate officers. A "little black book" containing girls' names and numbers was tucked away in a top-drawer corner of an antique roll-top desk. Comfortable, sturdy redwood stables housed four horses and their tack. Two working bird-dogs lived in an air-conditioned dog kennel on the edge of the property. A ground's keeper's house was situated a short sprint from the main house. One-hundred-ten healthy pecan trees and a fruit orchard of sand pear, fig, apple and persimmon trees surrounded the two houses. I chose to sleep on a big brass bed, next to a gas fireplace in a downstairs bedroom with my private bathroom. Buddy and Sam took two of the remaining four bedrooms. That first dark, dark night, I was lullabied with the whoo-whoo's of whippoorwills and a symphony of tree frogs. My deep dreams were shattered by howling screams of coyotes; I lay sleepless, watching deer scrounging pecans in the near orchard.

Buddy and a close relative purchased the Wilcox County property, which became New Covenant Fellowship, Inc.

We had been married for eight years; for five of those years, Ryan had been working for Sear's as an air conditioning/refrigeration repairman. We had purchased a Palm tree encircled home in a middle-class, family-filled neighborhood of Ft. Lauderdale and began our family with our son, Jason. After two years, Ryan had had enough of the humdrum of daily existence, his job, bills and responsibility. He wanted out of the system...but not via the Move. He wanted to move to Colorado and raise marijuana on a mountaintop.

The plan was to sell our home, get rid of stuff, move into a travel trailer, save money and move to the Colorado Rockies. We got as far as the selling our home and stuff, loading up our son with his Matchbox cars in a Ford Econoline, which pulled a U-Haul, trailer with what-was-left and headed to Colorado. We never made it past Georgia.

Buddy was informed of our plan to pull out and check out. He had purchased the New

Covenant property in Georgia but had not sold his Florida ranch home in Hollywood Hills. Buddy asked us if we would be willing to baby-sit the Georgia property until he had sold his home and moved up. It was a valid request, as the two story, pine built, plantation home was filled with valuable antique furniture, artwork and appliances. Unattended, it was a burglar's dream. We agreed to help.

Ryan was sporting a full beard, which made him look like somebody's rabbi. Beards were forbidden in the Move as a sign of hippie-style rebellion. Ryan intended to keep his beard to indicate he wanted nothing to do with the church.

The Mississippi group of 150 had already settled into the Ben Hill property. The women had opened a school in the restaurant building, using one big dining room as a one-room school, classes were separated by sheets hung from wire strung from wall to wall. Meals were cooked on the relinquished, commercial caste iron stove and served to farm residents in the main dining room of the former restaurant. Men and women were assigned daily schedules; children were in daycare school or on supervised work schedule. They were successfully operating a Move farm.

Our dark green Econoline grunted its way up the east coast of Florida and into Georgia. Thirteen miles south of Fitzgerald, Georgia, and twenty-five miles from Bowen's Mill, a puff of hot steam rose ominously from under the flat hood of the van. The van was exhausted and quit.

Grimly contemplating our limited options, Ryan called an emergency contact given to him by his father. Within an hour, two able men from the new Bowen's Mill community chained our vehicle and trailer to the back of a heavy farm truck, gave our son a Coke and towed us to the front door of the plantation house in Wilcox County. Exhausted and disappointed, without a car or food, we assumed we would be going to bed hungry.

Within an hour, Pat appeared to invite us to the communal meal at Bowen's Mill.

Pat and his wife were South Georgia natives. Years earlier, they had moved to Atlanta, became involved with the "Atlanta Body" of the Move and followed fellow parishioners to homestead in Alaska. This group of Deep South urbanites survived their first frigid Alaskan winter living in tents and eating

19

whale, moose meat, fish and blubber ice cream. Their community, near Fairbanks, would be known as The Land. During the 1977 Christmas holidays, Pat, his wife and four children returned to Fitzgerald to spend time with family. They never went back to the North, abandoning their belonging to deteriorate in cardboard boxes piled high in their rustic Alaskan cabin.

We went to dinner that night and every night following — and we attended the daily after-dinner singing and preaching, every night and every night following.

Buddy's Hollywood home sold within six weeks, freeing Buddy and Dottie to join us in Georgia. My close friend, Rose, also Buddy's personal secretary and girl-Friday, came with them. My husband's younger sister with her husband and daughter left their Ft. Lauderdale home and moved in making nine of us sharing the living quarters of what would be dubbed "The Big House".

Prompting a necessary decision, Buddy asked us if we were leaving to continue to Colorado, or were we staying on the farm. We stayed and flushed the last of our marijuana stash down the upstairs toilet.

Buddy soon opened the property to others within the Move who felt God was leading them out of the city. Many from the Hollywood group purchased mobile homes or built homes on the offered property officially forming the church of New Covenant Fellowship, Inc.

The members would own their homes, but the dirt was owned by the church, New Covenant Fellowship, Inc. Each family or member voluntarily contributed to a funded budget which paid for the garden, animal programs, communal building maintenance, common utilities and other farm expenses. Other than the five dinners per week, each home purchased their own food, paid their children's school fees and was responsible for their own finances.

New Covenant Fellowship became a fully functioning Move community with nearly ninety occupants.

Big House

People moved to the farms, lockstockandbarrel. At New Covenant, most had come with the suggested notion that we would work together to become self-sufficient by raising our own food and possibly generating our own electricity. Husbands and fathers had abandoned careers and businesses bringing financial savings to invest in "the Kingdom." Reality quickly arrived as their funds dwindled. Local jobs, scarce as they were, paid minimum wage. Women might have found a job sewing for Fitzgerald Underwear, waitressing at Shoney's or running a cash register at TGY or Piggly Wiggly. We women learned that we were more valuable on the farm to teach in the school, cook for corporate meals, raise our children, tend the garden and care for our own households. Necessity being the impetus, the men built their own businesses; they painted, they built, they repaired motors, they flew airplanes, they dug septic systems, they milled lumber, they plumbed, they worked wherever they found work. Except for my husband.

Buddy contended that God had told him he was to support us financially while my husband remained on the farm and continued to do manual farm work. Buddy supplied us with room and board in his own home for eight years. He later purchased our new mobile home, a new van and sustained us with a monthly "donation" for many more years.

In addition to my delegated farm duties, I lived Dottie's schedule. Our personal household items had either been sold or were packed in boxes stored in the attic above the farm shop. I took my turn preparing meals in the Big House kitchen, using Dottie's pots, pans and appliances. Every Friday, my assigned tasks were to clean our living area, polish the kitchen cupboards, shine the refrigerator inside and out, and mop the floor. My second child, ever the curious toddler, often crawled under my feet to investigate cupboard contents or pulled up on table legs scouting for goodies. On a so-far-so-good cleaning day, Dottie's revered brown-drip pottery, one-gallon pitcher which had been handed down from her mother, sat, ready and filled with sweet iced tea, near the kitchen table's edge. As "Oh, no!" flew out of my mouth, my pudgy little girl tottered and stretched for the pitcher handle, clasped it tightly and, under its full weight, toppled backward, clunking her curly-locked head soundly on my newly mopped floor. The entire gallon of sweet tea overwhelmed her as it splashed from the floor upward, splattering cupboards, countertops, the oven, refrigerator and chairs. Thankfully, Rose plucked her from the tea sea and removed her from the scene before the possibility of further incident.

Living in the Big House offered limited privacy. Conversations flowed easily through the wooden doors of all rooms. Our bedroom was over Buddy and Dottie's bedroom.

Even with advantage of being isolated upstairs, we could hear every snore, every grunt and every groan from below, as they could hear us. It was not uncommon for Dottie to greet me in the morning with, "Are you okay? I heard you walking around in the middle of the night."

Corporate life at New Covenant Fellowship centered around the needs of the larger farm family. Breakfast and lunch were taken at individual homes or at school. The entire community ate dinners together during the week and potluck on Sunday after a lengthy church service. Saturday was a free night.

Until the men built the New Covenant tabernacle to accommodate the then ninety of us for meals and meetings, we congregated in the limited space of the Big House living room. Every evening, metal folding chairs and six-foot folding tables scraped across the Tennessee peg-wood floor to be arranged for dining. Food was prepared in homes by a team of women who had been scheduled for meal preparation and transported to the Big House. We who lived in the Big House were fortunate to cook as one team and serve our meal directly from Dottie's kitchen without having to schlep hot, sloshing pans in the trunk of a car.

For one of our team's meals, I planned a hearty chicken soup, tossed salad and Rose's airy white dinner rolls. I boiled several fat whole chickens with garlic and celery to create my soup stock. After removing the chickens for boning, I tiptoed to strain the broth into a tall stock-pot set on the gas range. I dumped the shredded chicken, tossed in cut raw carrots, onions, and parsnips before allowing the fragrant brew to bubble contentedly for several hours with an occasional stir. Rose performed her magic as she mixed, kneaded and formed her weightless white rolls. As dinnertime approached, the aroma of fresh baking bread and chicken soup seeped into every nook and cranny of the Big House; salad, butter and pitchers of icy-cold tea were placed on each of the eight dining tables. A strong man carried the hot and heavy soup pot to a counter where, perched on a stool, I ladled each serving. Rose had not been able to locate the straw breadbaskets and heaped her delicate rolls into stainless steel bowls. I tilted the soup pot to save the last tasty dregs and there, drenched in chicken bits and carrots, peered the missing breadbaskets.

New Covenant Tabernacle

Inside New Covenant Tabernacle

Four horses roamed freely in the tall grasses of the pecan orchard: a fat, headstrong pinto mare; a mild-tempered quarter horse; a rambunctious palomino and an elderly gelding with severe sun allergies. A redwood stable with four roomy stalls and a tack room complete with saddles, harnesses, bits, blankets and grooming tools. Our city-bred children had high expectations of donning cowboy hat, boots and chaps, leaping on a horse and galloping out their frontier fantasies.

The four stalls were thickly carpeted in eighteen inches of hard-packed, manure sodden hay. The horses' hooves were in dire need of a farrier and their coats were filthy and fly-ridden. Childhood horseback riding lessons had left me with my own Annie Oakley reveries, none of which included shoveling horse poop. Nevertheless, I volunteered for the daunting task of caring for the four horses, hauling wheelbarrow loads of pungent hay to the compost pile, bathing each horse, scraping gunk from their hooves, untangling their unkempt tails and manes and plucking black flies from their ears.

The children from the three communities enjoyed the equine experience until the day sweat-bees swarmed from their nest underfoot the mount of my husband riding double with our five-year-old son. The heinous insects attacked the underbelly of the gentle quarter-horse. She bucked and jumped, the saddle slid, and the two guys were thrown roughly into the dirt. We waved our fond good-byes as the horses rode off into the sunset with new owners.

Two hunting dogs came with the farm. They were pointers, high strung, anxious, great in the field but not kid-friendly. It was an easy decision to ditch the dogs. The kennel was converted into a summer cannery in which we canned countless Mason jars of cut green beans, field peas and tomatoes, many of which rotted while waiting for the end of the world as we know it.

Aiming for self-sufficiency and steak, we purchased a small herd of beef calves-Brangus, a hybrid breed of Angus and Brahman. Our green-horns attempted to roundup the frisky calves to herd them into a corral for worming. The worming process required shoving a long surgical tube down a disinclined calf's throat, then pumping in meds. The calves had other plans for that day; they teamed up, jumped the rail fence and bounded gleefully to pasture.

We raised litters of piglets. Sows were sold as gilts or kept for breeding. Boars were fattened and frequently roasted, deeply buried in sand-covered pits for sumptuous pigpickin' feasts. Pigs are said to have the disposition closest to that of unredeemed man. Obese, arrogant, self-absorbed and egocentric, they shoved rudely for prime positions at the food trough. Often guilty of cannibalizing their own young, nursing sows were enclosed in tight quarters, to keep the piglets safe from being eaten or crushed by their oblivious, uncaring mother.

Our little boys were recruited to assist in pig births because their small, flexible hands could delve into a sow's birth canal to rescue a stuck piggie. Our little girls loved the soft, pink skin and sweet smell of newborn piglets, and often gathered them up and paraded around the farm with diapered piggies in blanket-lined doll buggies.

New Covenant owned ten acres of swampy land, ideal for growing sugar cane. To avoid the razor-sharp edges of the tall, slender stalks, we wore long sleeved shirts as we macheted the cane into rows. The cut cane was processed through a tractor-driven cane grinding mill. A vast, red-brick, wood-fired stove held two fifty-gallon iron pots of raw cane juice.

Freshly pressed cane juice was poured into the pots and cooked steadily, with constant stirring, until it condensed into a thick bubbling pungent syrup. Whole lemons were thrown into the finished concoction to temper the strong, molassesy flavor. The fire was extinguished, the hot syrup strained into quart Mason jars and labeled to be sold at conventions.

The cane-juice dregs were collected from the mill in a fifty-gallon drum. The filled drum of bubbling, fermenting draughts was trucked to the pig barn to be greedily guzzled by the snuffling swine. The inebriated pigs staggered drunkenly through their own feces seeking to exuberantly fornicate with one another or whatever else was in their path.

The people who worked the cane mill walked back-and-forth between the covered shelter of the steaming pots and cold, damp December weather. The conditions were ideal for creating bronchitis and pneumonia, illnesses which weakened the work force. Although the financial profits produced by the cane operation were great; the sugar cane mill was shut down after the second season.

Fried frog legs, a favored fare, are served with sides of cheesy grits and coleslaw in Southern restaurants. A New Covenant entrepreneur thought it a good idea for the community to invest in a frog program. The elders agreed, the frogs were purchased and released to the banks of a sizable pond adjoining the hog barn. Frogs are difficult to contain, and they hippity-hopped away from their pond to interbreed with native resident frogs. The population of long-legged, bug-eyed frogs increased until the buzzards could hardly keep the farm roads clear of flattened frog corpses. It was the end of the frog program.

Near a wooded perimeter, we erected a chicken coop, complete with brooding boxes enclosed within an eight-foot fence separating the barn fowl from woodland fauna. Since I had demonstrated strong poop-shoveling abilities, I was chosen for the weekly task of raking the chicken yard and replacing filthy brood-box bedding with clean hay. In the shadow of dawn, I slid my hand under the downy hens' bellies to snatch warm eggs and quickly learned that snakes also enjoyed the cozy warmth. Racoons easily manipulated the chicken-gate clasp, and sly foxes and bobcats crawled under or jumped over the fence to choose a fat dinner hen. A gun-toting volunteer took night sentry until the coop was moved to a more populous area of the farm.

Chickens can be as savage as their predators. One early morning, swinging the egg bucket, I announced my arrival with a booming rendition of a rooster's cock-a-doodle-doo. The hens cackled and crooned seductively anticipating a new man in town. The dominant White Leghorn rooster saw me as a threat and, talons poised forward, he flew toward my eyes. Instinctively, I whacked him soundly with the bucket, sending him spinning backward in front of the watching hens. My brother-in-law heard the screams of woman and fowl and came running to my rescue. He snatched the rooster around his scrawny neck and swung him around his head until the bird hung lifeless. His feathery form was stuffed into a gunnysack for later disposal. Within a few hours, the gunnysack was bouncing around and making angry rooster sounds. The ultimate deathblow came as an ax to the rooster's neck.

Older, lingering hens who ceased laying, were awarded a higher calling as chicken-potpie. Chicken slaughtering days were a depressing time of blood spouting, headless chickens careening soundlessly before dipped into a tub of boiling water, defeathered carved open, degutted, wrapped and frozen. My personal consensus was that the resulting tough, stringy, tasteless meat was not worth the effort and I did my best to avoid the entire messy affair.

From another community, New Covenant inherited two enormous mules, Neb and Dan. We figured we needed mules to pull plows when the world system collapsed, and fuel was scarce. The mules assumed that they had finally found retirement and tucked their heads at the sight of the heavy, brass-laden, double-harness, stubbornly refusing to budge. Neb and Dan contentedly grazed undisturbed through one summer until a penetrating sun ignited a dried mule paddy, spreading fire across the parched pasture. The mules were taken away to auction.

We were convinced that every self-sufficient farm deserved a soft, serene milk cow. We purchased Bess to supply us with fresh milk, curdy cheese and homemade ice cream. There was one woman on the farm who had previously milked a cow and she unwillingly became the chosen milkmaid. We were all stunned when our complacent cow raised up a hoof and brutally kicked the unsuspecting milk maid in the stomach.

We did not give up and shackled the cow's four legs for months of more ice cream.

When Bess succumbed to acute mastitis, the milkmaid did no mourning. There were other farm endeavors, other projects, other ideas to make money. As time continued, we lost interest in most — the work was too hard, it was time wasted, it was too expensive — we kept a smaller garden and fewer chickens and purchased milk from Piggly Wiggly.

Cows at the Stable

Cowboy Dreams

Since New Covenant had not prepared a garden plot for the first summer planting, it was decided that we would join our work force with the Ridge to plant, harvest and can. Men in long denim jeans and shirts harvested the garden during steamy summer mornings, bringing bushel baskets of vegetables to us women for processing.

A decrepit, red brick barbeque pit stood starkly against the backdrop of a crumbling, concrete swimming pool, a reminder of fun-filled summer gatherings once had at Bowen's Mill recreational center. Rusty, cast iron grates covered an unregulated wood fire on which we propped pressure cookers filled with seven quart-jars of freshly cut vegetables. Our children were forbidden to participate in the extremely hazardous working zone. Only once did a pressure cooker explode, spraying hot steam, broken glass and cut green beans high into the branches of pine trees banking House Creek. (Thankfully, no one was hurt)

New Covenant was eager to do our own gardening and canning. After we had met the budget, the elders chose a half-acre plot within the circle of mobile homes on which to plant rows and rows and rows of vegetables. The dog kennel was refashioned into a cannery lined with empty wooden shelves, two freezers and a closed screened area in which we washed, prepared the produce and processed the filled Mason jars in pressure cookers atop an electric kitchen range.

There were rows of field peas and English peas, each pregnant pod was handpicked into bushel baskets to be emptied on top of our dining tables for after-dinner shelling. Full bowls of peas were collected, refrigerated and taken to the cannery the next morning. A favorite summer image is that of rows of wide, wooden cannery shelves lined with steely-hatted, clear glass jars filled with bright green-peas.

Wheelbarrow loads of fire engine red tomatoes were pushed from the garden to the cannery to be blanched, peeled, canned whole or made into sauce. We savored our cannery lunches of home-baked bread, spread with Miracle Whip and topped with a fresh, juicy tomato slice. Any lone tomatoes left on the vines to rot became legitimate ammunition for tomato wars.

My husband was responsible for the plowing, tilling and fertilizing of our garden; his instinct was to go as organically as possible in the cheapest way possible. A local poultry farmer gave him a good deal on a self-loaded batch of fresh chicken manure. Leaving early to return before the noon sun, he arrived home with his pick-up bed brimming with odiferous, wet chicken poop. He stretched his long legs over the side of his truck to stand knee-deep in the foul, tarlike goo and shovel the stinky mess over the entire garden area. As the rising sun heated the earth, an unbearable stench wafted into our near homes. A few families fled to a Fitzgerald hotel and remained there until the nauseating odors dissipated. It took strong soap to rid Ryan's clothing of the smell and it was weeks before his truck would arrive ahead of its funk.

During one of Sam Fife's frequent visits, he surveyed a blank field on New Covenant property which adjoined a swampy cypress pond. Running his sinewy hand through his cropped hair, he growled, "You know, this would be a good place to plant a cornfield" Then he left. Believing Brother Sam always had the word of God on our behalf, my husband plowed the field and planted rows of sweet corn. Fed by the soggy grasses, the stalks grew to the sky spurting multitudes of healthy, fat ears of corn. As the silken tassels dried to black, pubic hairs, we knew it was time to harvest. In the cool of early dawn, wearing long sleeves to protect our arms, we ripped ears from the stalks piling them high into the back of the farm pick-up.

The corn was tossed into a growing mountain on the cannery lawn where we sat on upside-down buckets or low lawn chairs, each of us welded a machete or butcher knife to whack both ends off each ear. Often a fat, chubby corn worm would drop from an exposed end to nibble gently under the blouse of a task absorbed woman.

We wrapped the unhusked ears ten-to-a pack in newspaper to freeze for later winter use. We grated succulent ears into creamed corn, which froze into a gooey white tasteless paste. Steamed salted and buttered Silver Queen corn brought the taste of summer to many an October convention meal.

Somehow, we convinced ourselves that OUR corn was like no other and since God had blessed us with so much, we could make a profit by driving a truckload to the Jacksonville farmer's market. After all, it was Brother Sam who had endorsed the planting and he possessed the word of God. We loaded a Saturday morning corn picking into the farm truck and Ryan, Jason and I drove the three hours to market where we were directed to a small space between a score of corn-laden trucks.

I had prepared a packed breakfast for five-year-old Jason, which included a glass-lined thermos filled with cold milk. He hunched on the open tailgate to enjoy his rare outdoor meal and was nearly finished when he blurted, "Mom, thank you for putting ice in my milk. It made it really cold" Ice in his milk? I had not put ice in his milk. I grabbed the thermos to find shards of glass floating in the half-inch residual milk. In a controlled panic, leaving corn and husband Cobb behind, I dragged Jason to a pay phone at a 7/11 to call poison control. I was instructed to immediately feed him as much white bread as he could swallow and be watchful of fecal blood. Jason was delighted because I never had allowed him to eat "junky" white bread and afraid that I would change my mind, he quickly devoured an entire loaf of Wonder Bread. We returned to the truck, gave away the corn, discarded the thermos and drove back to the farm. (Jason was fine.)

Under the glow of the 2nd Quarter Moon, we planted New Covenant's front field in enormous Jubilee and smaller, seedless Crimson Sweet watermelons. Days before the Fourth of July, we tiptoed among the watermelon-vine maze, choosing ripened creamy yellow-bellied melons, carrying them on our shoulders to the waiting truck; often "busting one open" on the tailgate to share the sugary, deep-red heart before chunking the rest to the cows.

We grew lots of okra, a prolifically growing green pod covered with fine spines that cause intense itching when touched. We picked twice a day wearing elbow high rubber gloves and snipping each okra from its stem with small paring knives. Concealed by a can of diced tomatoes, okra is a slimy, boiled Southern delicacy to be spooned over buttery white rice. Okra is best when coarsely sliced and combined with chunks of sweet onions and green tomatoes, breaded in a salted cornmeal-flour mixture then fried to a crispy delight. We could not pick enough okra to satisfy the fried okra cravings of the communal family.

An ambitious okra-loving minister breezed through the farm and dropped the suggestion that a large field of okra could be a big money maker for New Covenant. His innovative plan was to install a rotating sprinkler system, which would spray as we picked. The shower would keep us cool and reduce the okra itch. His name was not Sam Fife, and, consequently, we ignored his idea.

Gardening was hard, hot work and growing fresh vegetables was a gamble, but I surely miss those tomato sandwiches and watermelon hearts.

Included in the land purchase for New Covenant was a pecan orchard containing one-hundred-ten nut producing trees. Although, we were a nut farm, we did not have a clear concept of how to manage the orchard and harvest the nuts. We learned that we had to have our crop bagged and ready for sale by the beginning of the winter holidays or lose out to our experienced competitors.

Dusty spring blooms birthed clusters of stony, green pecan nubs which slowly evolved into a green, husked nuts. By late October, the green husks dried to a dark brown, split and separated from the mature nut. The ripe nuts stubbornly clung to their branches until, strength gone, they fell to the ground where squirrels and deer gobbled them up.

Our task was to harvest them from the trees before they fell.

We gazed up at the heavily laden branches wondering how to coax the mature nuts from the towering trees. Someone told us the nuts would have to be shaken from the trees. With that information, our largest, nimblest men clambered up into the stretching limbs, hung on tightly and bounced up-and-down on the branches. A volley of nuts, twigs and autumn leaves peppered the ground while the rest of us, mostly women in long denim skirts, dropped to our knees and floundered to collect the pecans into numerous 5-gallon buckets.

From the damp chill of fall dawn to the hour before supper, this was our daily activity for nearly four weeks.

The harvested pecans were moved to our dining hall where, after our communal dinner, the tables were cleared, and the buckets of nuts were dumped into the center of each of the eight large round tables. Un-ripened nuts in green husks were discarded while the brown-shelled nuts were individually hand-cracked. The tasty meat was pulled from its thin shell with narrow, metal nut picks to be sorted into two piles, whole half pieces or broken nut bits. The piles were gathered into large bowls and poured onto cookie sheets for a final quality inspection. A vagrant fragment of hard shell could easily crack a tooth. Nuts contaminated by black insect bites could bitter baked goods. Pristine nut meats were loosely measured into clear plastic bags, weighed, sealed and frozen.

Bowen's Mill conventions were our most successful pecan sales venues. Pounds of bagged pecans were purchased and hand-carried to the Alaskan and Canadian wilderness farms to be baked into nut filled, delectable baked goods for their own use or to be sold to bakeries and restaurants. New Covenant pecans traveled to Move communities and city groups in Asia, Europe, South America, Australia, Africa and beyond.

By our second pecan season, we had purchased a pecan tree shaker, a wide, sturdy belt to be wrapped around a pecan tree and anchored to the John Deere tractor. When the tractor clutch was engaged, the belt vibrated the tree, and the nuts hailed to the ground. Our bountiful pecan harvests funded the purchase of a commercial pecan sorting and cracking machine.

We learned to lay sheets of visqueen under each tree to catch the rain of shaken nuts. The nut-full visqueen was folded and dragged to an open shed where a fan blew chaff, leaves and twigs from the gathered nuts. The separated nuts were steadily streamed into the sorting and cracking machine before being taken to the dining hall for shelling, sorting and bagging.

My husband, wearing only a motorcycle helmet for protection, drove the John Deere from tree to tree, wrapped the belt around their girth, then jumped back on the tractor seat to crank up the shaker. His goals were to keep far ahead of the pecan-picker-upper's and to finish the pecan harvest as quickly as he could.

I was not among the pickers the morning a topmost limb crashed on his back, sending him tumbling to the ground. Two men shouldered him to the back door of our doublewide trailer, laid him on our living room carpet and removed his shirt. He had been hit squarely across his back below his neck, but, thankfully, he was fully conscious; although, his upper back and shoulders were swelling, and bits of bark were deeply imbedded in his skin. Emergency situations necessitated intuition, skill and prayer for the nearest hospital was fifteen miles away. I cleaned his back, applied ice, then rubbed a potion into his back which reduced the swelling. Ryan was back on the tractor the next day. Years later, bits of pecan bark continued to surface through the skin on his back.

Pecan harvest was just another scheduled event as was winter garden, summer garden, canning, chicken slaughtering, daily dinner prep, school, kitchen clean-up, church services, Bible studies, conventions and maintenance of common areas.

As our children grew up, graduated from our high school and left the farm, our labor force dwindled until we could no longer manage the workload of harvesting pecans. New Covenant's pecan equipment was given to a Move community in Mexico, who are successfully supported by their pecan industry.

New Covenant's pecan orchard of one-hundred-ten nut-producing trees was leased to a commercial pecan grower.

Shaking a Pecan Tree

The Pecan Shaker

Picking up Pecans

There was a never-ending stream of personalities that flowed through the doors of the Big House. Some came for dinner, some came for convention, some came to visit, and some came to live.

We were the last resort for Bill, a former traveling minister and former leading elder of a Move community in New England. Bill was known as a drunk, a drug addict, a thief and an ex-con and somehow the father ministry had determined that Buddy's guest house was the perfect haven for Bill and my husband was his perfect custodian. Colossal and loud, he reeked of garlic, spoke multiple languages, had a photographic memory and played any musical instrument at first touch. While in prison, he had become an uncontested chess master, a talent he readily shared with my children. It was not uncommon for Bill to lead a man to Christ in the back room of a store, then five-finger goods on his way out.

On a fall Saturday afternoon, I invited Bill to accompany me and the children to a youth rodeo in another town. Nearing our destination, we stopped at a gas station to purchase snacks, gas-up and use the facilities. Arriving at the rodeo, we found seating on grey metal folding-chairs. As Bill sat down next to me, I noticed a wet stain spreading from his back pocket into a pink puddle on his chair. When I questioned him, he jumped up and, shamefaced, asked to find a bathroom. As he ambled off, I daintily touched my finger to the pink puddle and took a whiff. Cough syrup. He had stolen a bottle of cough syrup from the gas station, shoved it into his back pocket, forgot and sat on it.

For our wedding anniversary we had been gifted a lovely bottle of red wine which I had stashed deep inside a work boot on my husband's side of our bedroom closet. I was flabbergasted when Bill sheepishly mumbled, "You know that bottle of wine you had put in Ryan's boot...?" It was gone.

Hoping to elude Bill's discovery of my children's cherry-flavored cough syrup, I had hidden the small bottle high on the ledge inside our attic access. Bill sniffed it out, drank it, leaving just enough red liquid to color a refill of water.

Money for our school was raised by monthly fundraisers of talent shows, piano concerts or bake sales held in the New Covenant tabernacle. A large, open donation container perched atop an upright piano near the entryway. After one event, we were dismayed to find the container nearly empty. Bill helped in the search for the alleged thief before admitting it was he who had taken the funds.

I was assigned to manage Bill's prescription medicines and chaperone his pharmacy visits. After suspecting that he had double-dipped at two pharmacies, I confronted him while we stood alone in Buddy's office. I suddenly found myself pinned to the wall by Bill's strong left hand as he poised his enormous right fist inches from my nose. I quietly spoke, "Go ahead, hit me, Bill. You want to hit me. Just do it." His gigantic arms trembled, he dropped his fist, turned away and left the room. I nearly collapsed with relief.

While pregnant with my third child, I experienced painful leg swelling which I controlled with diet and afternoon rests on our couch. With my legs propped on pillows, I completed a cross-stitch sampler while Bill played his guitar and sang to me from across the room. As I labored painfully in my bedroom, he sat on the air conditioner outside my window, quietly strumming and singing. I gave him my deceased father's watch. He honored me, and I trusted him.

During Bill's time with us, we acquired a young policeman from British ruled Hong Kong named Steven Kow. While attending a Move convention in Hong Kong, Steven approached Buddy to confess his homosexual affair with a prominent Chinese pastor.

Buddy invited Steven to live with us at the Big House for his deliverance and recovery. I arranged a second bed for Steven in the guesthouse with Bill.

Steven's first night at New Covenant set the tone for the remainder of his days with us. Attempting to manipulate the unfamiliar shower plumbing, he inadvertently pulled the handle out of the wall creating a fire-hydrant gush of water. Unable to control his mirth, Bill burst into our living room to summon help. Ryan rushed to find the five-foot-two, ninety-four-pound, naked Chinaman desperately trying to stop the geyser with the palm of his hand.

Steven gave us daily updates of Bill's personal habits earning him the title of Hong Kong Phooey. They were the ultimate odd couple, the big, burly Russian and the scrawny, wiry Chinaman.

We endured Bill's continued antics, until, spiritually spent, we could do no more for him. He left us to join a prison ministry in North Georgia, but regularly returned for conventions, often bringing me a carload of day-old bread for the convention kitchen.

It was after Bill's death that I was dismayed to learn more truth about him. While the head elder of the New England community, he had misused his authority to abuse and molest weaker members and children. The ministry had quietly closed his farm and he had been sent to us without disclosure. I was shocked that ministry had allowed him to live intimately with us and our children. It was a confusing moment for me because I had genuinely cared for the man. He had rarely shown animosity to any of us and had never hurt the children.

It was the Move's way to deal with sexual predators.

While in community, we lived "by faith" believing that if we needed something, God would provide it, somehow. It worked for me.

It was our fifteenth wedding anniversary, we had three kids, and we had no money. I had earlier resigned myself to "it was just another anniversary" and proceeded with my day. I opened the bathroom cupboard to grab toothpaste and found a stack of quarters wavering against the eye wash bottle.

$5.00 in quarters? Wonder where it came from. Maybe my husband moved them from his jeans. Shrugging, I scooped them up and dumped them into my purse. Finders keepers.

I opened my dresser drawer for a pair of clean undies. There hidden in full sight between my red and white polka dots and black lace was a sandwich bag loaded with quarters. $10.00 more. Now who would open my underwear drawer?

My curiosity was piqued. I tactfully questioned my children, without revealing my found fortune, "Did anyone leave any money laying around?" Noooooooo. Good, it was still mine.

Putting out breakfast, I bumped against a broken stack of quarters chilling in the fridge behind the butter dish. There was yet another pile occupying an empty Starbuck's mug in the cupboard. Full mug in hand, I was pondering the money mystery when I saw a glossy note taped to a quarter tower flanking my blue African violet. It read, "Happy Anniversary!"

An angel had decided to celebrate our anniversary!

I knew where I wanted to go. Although an hour-and-a-half drive to Albany, Gargano's Italian Restaurant was my favorite restaurant. Ryan agreed on my choice, Grandma agreed to keep the children and we were off with a baggie full of quarters.

At 74, Mama Suzi (Gargano) had survived her beloved Sicilian husband to become the heart, soul and chief cook-and-bottle-washer of their famous Italian restaurant which opened in 1968 (and is still operating at another location). Accompanied by a gypsy violinist, Mama Suzi waltzed daintily through the candlelit tables while balancing a full bottle of Chianti atop her tight bun hairdo. At 4' 10", she made me tall.

Devout Catholics, Mama Suzi and her daughter attended daily mass before opening the restaurant. She was curious as to my religious position. Opening her clouded dark eyes widely, she reacted with squeals of "Oh, my!" as I shared stories of the three Bowen's Mill communities.

Over the years of visits for special occasions, Mama Suzi and I became friends. Impressed by my culinary interest in her food, she permitted me access to the inner workings of her kitchen to learn the basics of sauces and dough. I watched fatback rendering slowly in a heavy pot on top of a low gas flame before freshly crushed basil leaves and whole fragrant garlic cloves were added to complete the sizzling aromas. With a long wooden spoon, I stirred crushed tomatoes and one can of thick, crimson tomato paste into the medley. This was her pasta sauce which Mama Suzi ladled over her homemade spaghetti which hung white and limp on racks near pots of boiling water.

Her pizza sauce began with freshly chopped oregano and garlic simmered in virgin olive oil to draw out and blend the intense flavors that only Gargano's pizza had. Balancing a circle of pizza dough on her small, pudgy fist Mama Suzi threw it high, watching it spin and stretch to fill the cornmeal dusted pizza pans waiting near hot brick ovens.

To be allowed to view her art was a rare privilege for which I am ever grateful.

Mama Suzi culminated our visits to Gargano's by ceremoniously sashaying from the depths of her kitchen to hand us a large cardboard box filled with fresh, warm bread, a bottle of Chianti and maybe a pizza "for the kids." She leaned up high on her toes to plant a wet Italian kiss on our cheeks to let us know we were "always welcome."

We shared Gargano's with Bowen's Mill and soon others were making the drive for celebratory meals, dropping my name for recognition and hugs from Mama Suzi. She understood that some from the farms would "absolutely never drink alcohol of any sort, ever, anywhere." Although, she courteously refrained from offering them wine, it did not keep her from sending me a brown paper bag containing a bottle of Chianti and a loaf of fresh, crusty bread. "Justa be careful wid dis, please. Its'a present for my Cara."

The Gargano's were known to the homeless as compassionate, generous folk who fed them through the backdoor of the kitchen. It was no surprise for Mama Suzi to become enamored with a tall, long-bearded old man and his tiny, faithful dog. After feeding him well, she asked him if he would be interested in a clean bed at a church. Of course, he was. She knew who to call. Despite being usually dubious of those who "came in off the road," we could not refuse her request.

Arriving in the Gargano's chauffeur driven black Cadillac with her daughter, Mama Suzi sat against a back door, frantically fanning herself with a cologne-soaked hanky. An unkempt, grisly man and his filthy little dog sprawled on the seat next to her. The purpose of the hanky became obvious as the man exited with the stench of a rank dumpster.

This was no social call. The Gargano's said their hellos and good-byes before escaping in a cloud of Cadillac exhaust. We stared at the man and his dog standing in our driveway as he and his dog stared at us.

My husband and Bill (the Russian) bathed the man in a tub, draining the water three times before the water ran clear. I could hear the man complain that they were "washing the sunshine off his body." After a haircut, shave and a full meal, the man refused a bed; he left, walking on down the highway with his little dog. We never even knew his name.

In what was to be her last tribute of affection, Mama Suzi prepared a spaghetti meal for over 200 of the farms' residents. She and I worked side-by-side in the convention's commercial-sized kitchen, rendering pork fat, simmering spices and browning pounds of finely ground beef to finish her fabulous pasta sauce. With buttered garlic bread and a huge salad, it was a celebration culminating with Mama Suzi twirling on the lawn to a gypsy tune with a quart-jar of non-offensive pickles balanced on her head.

Mama Suzi's daughter died suddenly, and, to our sorrow, she soon followed her daughter to eternity. The original Gargano's Restaurant closed, the building torn down, and a second Gargano's, operated by Suzi's estranged son, opened on the other side of town.

It was just not the same.

Mama Suzi's Dance

Our local medical options were limited to two dentists, a handful of general practitioners and no pediatrician. We would sarcastically comment about our experiences at Fitzgerald's sole hospital: "There is a good chance you may come out sicker than when you went in. If you even come out at all."

Whenever one of my children was ill, I was able to leave them home with a family member while I taught at the school. However, there was the time when a young Jason caught a flu bug with a high fever and the only person in the Big House was Sam Fife. Sam attempted to ease my maternal anxiety with calming words of, "Don't worry about him. I am here. I will pray with him." Uneasily, I left them sitting together in the kitchen. At first chance, I called the doctor from school and made the earliest appointment before returning home.

Sam met me at the door, "Jason and I prayed, and he is healed." I was not as assured and loaded Jason into the van for the twelve-mile drive to town. Sam's parting words rang hotly in my ears, "You are wasting your money by taking him to the doctor. He is fine."

After listening, looking and prodding, the doctor announced, "I find nothing wrong with the boy. He may have been sick, but he has made a very quick recovery." Sam merely chortled when I admitted the healing.

Sons of God did not go to doctors. Illness was either punishment for sinful living or it was an opportunity for God to be glorified through a miraculous healing. Doctors were for the "babes in Christ," the spiritually immature lacking the stronger faith for a healing or the fortitude to battle an illness. I never disputed the logic. I would rather be considered as "spiritually mature" than "too poor to afford a doctor."

When Dr. Dora Jackson, pediatrician, opened her office in town, I was curious and made a newborn appointment for my second born-at-home infant. Dr. Dora flip-flopped my baby around on the cold steel table as if she were examining a raw Thanksgiving turkey; pushing; poking; checking crevices, ears, eyes and gums. Her questions rolled as her hands and eyes inspected. "Where was she born? At home? Hmmmmm. Who was the attending doctor? None? Hmmmmmm. Well, looks like she made it just fine."

More from Bowen's Mill began to join her clientele, building her interest in the three communities until she showed up unannounced for an early Sunday church service. It was difficult not to watch her reactions as we raised our hands, danced at our seats and blurted the incomprehensible jargon of tongues. Dr. Dora became a regular attendant.

Before graduating from medical school, Dora Jackson had committed herself to serve her native town of Fitzgerald. Her father's untimely, sudden death sent her into a spiraling depression from which she desperately sought escape. Her growing association with the people of Bowen's Mill provided her with a safe social life and Christian solace from her personal storm. She became our doctor. No injury was too minor, no patient too poor and no tragedy too serious for Dr. Dora's healing hands as she ministered medically to all of us.

On Dr. Dora's advisement, a pediatric surgeon had performed a tonsillectomy on our youngest, Joy. On the tenth day after surgery, Joy attended a children's party, chowing down on Dorito's, cake and soda. Newly energized after her convalescence, she was the first to dive for a raining piñata, ending up at the bottom of a pile-up of candy-crazed kids. That night she tapped my sleeping shoulder, complaining of a bellyache before bolting to the toilet and vomiting blood— lots of blood. A hot blade of fear sliced through my sleepy mind as I leapt from bed while shrieking for my husband. He dialed Dr. Dora's home number as I rehearsed my Red Cross First Aide class of thirty years prior. "If the face is red, raise the head. If the face is pale, raise the tail." I lay her down, raised her legs and began feeding her ice chips, praying that the bleeding would stop.

Dr. Dora quietly entered our home, careful not to awaken my other two children. After assessing Joy's condition, she phoned the surgeon, loaded us into her van and sped toward the designated hospital, a long seventy-five-mile drive. I sat on the seat behind Dora with my child's head cradled in my lap, dropping ice chips into her mouth and chanting a scriptural mantra: "The Lord will never leave you nor forsake you."

A gurney met us at the emergency entrance and scooted Joy to the waiting surgeon, who had prepped for an immediate cauterization of a suspected lesion in her throat. As he peered intently behind her mouth, his welcomed words were, "The bleeding has stopped making no need to cauterize her throat. She probably needs blood, but, because of her age, I am hesitant to put her at risk of infection." Instead, he admitted her to a brief hospital stay while her blood level replenished.

I cuddled with her on the crisp white bed sheets through three days of receiving guests and gifts and watching countless carnal cartoons.

Dora Jackson eventually entered a relationship with Chuck, a handy-man from Florida who lived at the Ridge. Dr. Dora was an essential member of the Bowen's Mill communities, and it was highly unlikely that the elders would interfere with their possible marriage. The elders wanted her there. As expected, they wed and set-up house in a mobile home at New Covenant where they raised a son and daughter. Chuck was the stay-at-home dad while Dora continued practicing locally and on the three communities.

One very sad morning, with her children in their early teens, our doctor's husband suffered a massive heart attack and died. This second event of great loss and deep sorrow crumbled her. She clutched at sanity while continuing in her medical ministry to the communities and town. Her weight soared as her heart plummeted. She and her two children made a transition to a California community where she became involved in a state funded medical clinic. Her relentless struggle against health issues eventually ended with her own death, leaving her two children to independently secure their lives.

As the Move aged, cancer and other illnesses ravaged communities, the erroneous notion of gauging spirituality by number of doctor visits was discarded. Although they could still present medical decisions to the elders, people were encouraged to independently decide their own course of health care.

During the 1980's, the traveling ministry began proselytizing in Hong Kong while indulging in the low costs of electronics, custom made suits and Rolex watches. They were introduced to a popular preacher named Sam Fan who was a Buddha of a man with a roly-poly face and a following of undirected young men. Being a visionary, Sam Fan saw his relationship with the Americans as a golden opportunity to widen his influence and increase his offerings. Shining his ever-present smile, Sam Fan turned on his charm and gained an invitation to come-on-over to the United States, stay in Buddy's home and join the traveling ministry tours.

We at the Big House were delighted to receive the cheerful Chinaman who enjoyed cooking, cleaning and giggling with us ladies. We were the ones who catered to visiting ministry; Sam Fan catered to us.

He loved to shop and asked to accompany me on weekly shopping forays into Fitzgerald. With my pink frocked toddler in tow, we entered Fred's Department Store, the original Main Street five-and-dime offering everything from toothpaste to kitchenware, tools, toys and socks heaped high in waist-level wooden bins. Tin buckets strategically placed on the hardwood floor caught raindrops dripping through cracks in the patched ceiling. A vintage cash register pinged and dinged as the solitary proprietor tallied customers' purchases. Far in the back of the store was a grimy, swinging door opening into an overloaded storeroom and a one-seater restroom with enough space to sit, stand and wash one's hands in the tiny, stained ceramic sink-bowl

My gorgeous, chocolate-brown-eyed baby sat primly in the seat of the metal shopping cart, bubbling and cooing as she stretched for colorful wares beyond her reach. Pushing the metal buggy through the cluttered isles, I kept one hand firmly on hers while devoting my full attention to a scribbled grocery list. Sam Fan was occupied elsewhere admiring the vast inventory of Chinese goods.

My adorable baby girl suddenly emitted a dreadful trumpeting of sounds followed by a ghastly odor of rotting eggs. A violent eruption of brown spray spewed from all sides of her diaper, drenching me, the cart, the stuff in the cart and the floor with foul residue. There was a second of stunned silence as awareness crept in. We were twelve miles south of home, my adult companion was a single Chinese male, and Fred's limited facilities did not include a changing table. Nevertheless, I snatched her from her seat and holding her far from my body, I grabbed a toddler sundress from a nearby rack called out a quick explanation to Sam Fan and fled to the bathroom. I somehow managed to bathe her, paper-towel my blouse and redress her before pushing open the door to face the mephitic mess I had left behind. Amazingly there stood Sam Fan, smiling, his hand resting on an unsoiled shopping cart parked on a spotless floor and refilled with fresh items. He said, "I cleaned it up for you."

Sam Fan had a deep secret that was incongruous with Move doctrine. He was a homosexual and had had an affair with a young man in his parish. The young man confessed the "inordinate" relationship to Buddy and Sam Fan was barred from preaching to Move congregations until he agreed to be delivered from homosexual demons. After refusing an exorcism, he was shunned by the Move and returned to Hong Kong.

Sam Fan ultimately succumbed to AIDS. Move ministry firmly asserted it was God's punishment for his sexual preference.

I missed his cheerful countenance.

There is only one block home at New Covenant Fellowship; it was custom built for an elderly couple whose only connection to the Move was their son, a resident elder at New Covenant. We received them warmly and soon ensconced Mr. and Mrs. CG, Sr. in the role of farm grandparents. As life would have it, cancer took his wife shortly thereafter, leaving the heartbroken CG, Sr. to the watch-care of the community.

In his previous life, CG, Sr. had owned a Bible bookstore in his New England hometown. He reopened the business to sell Bibles, Bible cases and Christian literature from his New Covenant home. Without the internet, it was the only Bible bookstore within a ninety-mile radius of the farm, and the only one patronized by the three Bowen's Mill communities. I still own a zippered, nylon, pocketed Bible case which I purchased from CG, Sr.'s Family Books.

When PE was added to our school curriculum, I was delegated to take the girls PE class. Being that sport games were still forbidden, I had planned to occupy the class time with calisthenics, long hikes or short jogs through the woods behind the school. I avoided all ball games, for though I had often played alongside my two brothers, I was wary of any ball soaring toward me. I figured I'd never have to teach a ball sport at Bowen's Mill.

Unbeknownst to me, the high school girls made an appeal to the principal that they be allowed to play softball, and, amazingly, the motion was approved! I was frantic, I was not familiar with the rules, we had no equipment and I really did not want to play softball. Through his many stories, I had learned that CG, Sr. had once been a high school softball coach; I swiftly ran for his assistance. The gangly, eighty-year-old worked with me every week before class, reciting softball rules as he taught me how to hold the bat, pitch, catch and hit. With CG, Sr., at my back, I became a fearless girls' softball coach to an enthusiastic, talented team.

As physical limitations overtook his body, CG, Sr. asked me to gradually take control of Family Books, an easy request for a fervent bibliophilic. I grabbed at the opportunity to familiarize myself with various publishing houses, book sellers, authors and Bible producers. I learned the difference between bonded leather, genuine leather and Moroccan leather. I discovered that the only difference between a Harlequin paperback and a Christian romance novel was mention of angels, God and prayers. The forty-five- year-old FAMILY BOOKS sign was moved from CG, Sr.'s front porch to mine.

CG, Sr.'s mortal body faded as age and disease claimed his health. He became bedridden and was miserable about his inability to continue life. Visiting him became most distressful as he pleaded with me to remove him from his bed and take him "out of here." The day came when he begged no more and resigned himself to the Lord. His only request to me was the repeated recitation of Psalm 23—again and again, I quoted the familiar scripture until my tongue dried, and tears flowed down my cheeks. One morning, he slipped quietly away.

I continued the Family Books legacy until I had overextended my customers' credit and could not pay the store's bills. I no longer play softball, but I can still distinguish between genuine, Moroccan and bonded leather Bibles.

"Not-from-the-Move" visitors commonly appeared unannounced at a Bowen's Mill Convention meeting or to a regularly scheduled service held on any of the three farms. From the mountains of North Carolina came a sizeable group of stout, bearded men; unadorned women in ankle-length denim skirts and their orderly offspring. They settled children, Bibles and snacks in chairs at-the-back-near-a-bathroom position of the Convention Tabernacle. On the first chord of the opening praise session, the men rose to their full height, stepped away from their families and whooped, stomped, hopped and spun like a troupe of ambling circus bears veiled in a rising cloud of sawdust. The dancing bears soon tired of the epoch hours of redundant oration and did not return to another convention.

A two-story, wood-framed Hospitality House was built on Convention grounds with pine logged and milled on the property. Originally, as the home of the convention administrator and his wife, it also housed the Bowen's Mill Convention Center office, a kitchen, living room, two bedrooms and one bath downstairs; and two bedrooms and one bath upstairs. When the couple relocated, it became accommodations for ministerial guests from all nine continents. It was our duty to transcend cultural boundaries to make their stay as comfortable as we could.

Nevertheless, guests at the Hospitality House oftentimes had experiences beyond our control. Brother Eliezer was a pastor from the Dominican Republic who often traveled with my father-in-law as his Spanish translator (a duty which granted free travel and a percentage of collected offerings). Placed in the Hospitality House, he was snoozing, mouth wide open, in an oversized Lazy Boy under a ceiling fan. I was standing nearby when I saw something fall from the ceiling fan directly into his gaping mouth. Brother Eliezer coughed, gagged and opened his eyes before spitting a fat, white maggot into his palm. I quickly replaced the worm with a cookie and hot coffee, comforted Brother Eliezer with a smile and flushed the offensive intruder. It was later discovered that a squirrel had been trapped above the ceiling, died and decayed directly over the ceiling fan.

African pastors from the depths of the dark continent would arrive in the U.S. carrying only one bag. Scrounging unused luggage from church members, they stuffed the empty cases with Atlanta thrift store purchases to clothe their own impoverished flock. It was not unusual for one pastor and his wife to accumulate half-a-dozen suitcases crammed with clothing, shoes and baby items. Since the airline baggage limit was two checked bags, pieces of heavily packed luggage were often stashed in a stairwell closet until the next plane to Africa.

Most guest ministry preferred to board at the Big House, for it was as close to Buddy Cobb as one could get. I and the others who lived with Buddy were expected to treat all guests with Christian hospitality; cooking, cleaning, doing their laundry and meeting their needs with a smile. In return, I often persuaded them to share their personal culinary secrets. A Chinese pastor showed me how to bone a raw chicken before stuffing it with savory Chinese rice: "Don't think about taking the bones out of the chicken; think about taking the chicken off the bones." From a Mexican minister I gleaned a spicy salsa sauce and the trick to rolling a perfect tortilla, an essential talent for a good wife. I became less inclined to coax after a Cajun chef fried shrimp in an iron skillet and left the kitchen drenched in sticky, cooking grease.

Summertime brought those who wished to experience first-hand community living while helping with garden chores, construction of new buildings or convention prep work. We at the Big House were always glad to share our workload with any fresh strength. All of us females fell in love with the Crocodile Dundee twang of the cute twenty-three-year-old Aussie guy who arrived wearing "illegal" short-shorts. We boarded him, fed him, cleaned his room and did his laundry while he worked alongside the guys. On a crazed impulse, I chose a bright white pair of his bikini underwear as the canvas for a colorfully painted barnyard scene on which I drew spotted cows, pink pigs, a horse and half-a-dozen chickens running across his crotch area and around to his bum. Using needle and thread, I sewed shut the leg openings before folding the keepsake pair into his pile of clean laundry. I had to ask him before he blushingly admitted he had found them. Sadly, his visa was not extended.

Because of the farms' proximity to Highway 129, some guests wandered off the highway as a divine blessing or a demonic curse. While walking the narrow path crossing House Creek Bridge, I watched as a sun-bleached black van veered from the road to screech to a stop in the school parking lot. I cautiously approached the vehicle, half expecting to see a kidnapped victim's face screaming against its darkly tinted windows. Suddenly, the driver's door swung open to exit a long-haired wisp of a girl who raced to the back of the van to fling open the two doors. Using two metal canes, a three-foot-tall woman fumbled her way to the crumbling black-top before continuing a vicious argument with her companion. I decided to introduce myself.

They were two exhausted, famished women on their way to nowhere. Realizing that they had landed on church property, they asked to be fed. Bowen's Mill Christian Center does not turn away the hungry. I guided them to the nearest lunch-table after which they were offered needed showers and clean beds in a women's dorm.

To our exasperation, the ill-matched wanderers continued to scrap, argue and torment one another until, finally, the long-haired girl drove away in her van, leaving elfin Kay behind. Having no other place to go, Kay conceded that we were her saviors.

Our school had been collecting computer equipment in high hopes of introducing our high-schoolers to current technology. All we lacked was a qualified computer teacher. Although Kay had no teaching experience, we were thrilled to discover that she was an impressive computer geek.

The high schoolers colluded to test the diminutive faculty addition with harmless pranks and small annoyances, which frequently sent her complaining to the principal. Our principal responded with spontaneous classroom appearances, but always found the students sitting demurely before their computers and their eyes focused on their hapless teacher. Ultimately, Kay had her effective revenge.

My son came home lamenting about the stern, time-consuming requirements of her term project for each student to create a unique web page. I remember that his contained much text which, when completed, was centered perfectly, top and bottom, left and right. After days of fine tuning, the students breathed a collective sigh of relief as they left their finished pages for Kay's grading. At the beginning of their next class time, the kids anxiously turned on their assigned computers, opened their page and watched incredulously as letters and images funneled into the center of the page to slide into a reckless pile below the bottom border. Kay had finally earned the fond respect and friendship of her pupils. Leaving a valuable legacy and many friends, Kay left community to regain her life "in the world."

Church networking often attracted "outer court" preachers who found their way to the Bowen's Mill pulpit. Their attempts to captivate us with demonstrations of signs and wonders often provided us with welcomed entertainment. I was particularly amused by a healer who claimed that God would cure all ills through the drinking of one's own urine. Thirty dollars bought a thirty-minute health consultation in which he listened, diagnosed and inevitably prescribed the pee tonic. The thirty dollars also included a follow-up blood test in which blood was dripped onto a white sheet of paper and faxed to the good healer. His analysis of the faxed specimen would determine prognosis and the need of further treatment. Although, I did not, quite a few of the brethren paid their thirty dollars to consult with him and later faxed their blood to his number. I do not recall anyone receiving a response.

During my thirty-plus years in community, I met and hosted thousands of guests in our home, at the Big House and at the Bowen's Mill conventions. My family was often inconvenienced, taken advantage of and ill-used. Nevertheless, the experiences made us tolerable of others, grateful for what we had and flexible in any situation. And sometimes it was great fun.

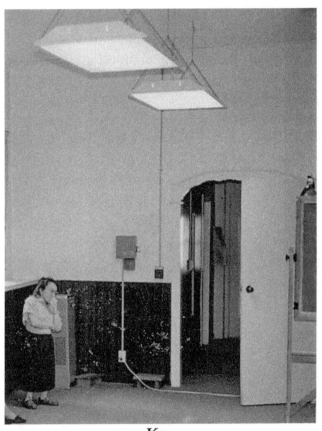

Kay

By September 1978, the Bowen's Mill school was in operation with about 85 students, grades K-12, a handful of teachers and a principal. Classes were held in the aforetime restaurant and hotel buildings located on Highway 129 and adjacent to House Creek. The men converted the commercial kitchen area and two large dining rooms into multi-grade classrooms and an assembly room; four private dining rooms became smaller classrooms.

One of the elders had had a dream in which he saw me illuminated by hundreds of twinkling lights. He felt the twinkling lights were children, and that I was anointed to become a teacher, and, thus, in September 1978, Miss Cara became an elementary teacher at the Bowen's Mill school.

It was unlike any classroom experience I had encountered, either as a pupil or a teacher. When the fall term began, there were no curriculum or materials, pencils or paper. I stood before nine elementary students in a 12x12 room with two windows, one door (which I was not permitted to open during class) and no air conditioning or heat. Outside my room was a big room which was divided into classes by sheets hanging from wall to wall. Nursery and daycare were housed in the same building. The noise level fueled by the different classes and crying babies was disconcerting.

Infant caregivers suppressed a baby's crying by placing their palm over the mouth and nose of the baby repeatedly until the infant lost her breath and ceased crying. I vowed never to put my children in daycare.

The elders had appointed a diabetic and alcoholic Army veteran as our principal. Striving to keep distance between his boozy breath, students and teachers, he would line us and our students against a wall for morning praise song assembly. Emulating his days as a drill sergeant, his lanky frame strode up and down the line, pausing to glare intently if he found one of us not singing, clapping and raising our hands to praise the Lord. A non-participating teacher was publicly and loudly admonished; pupils were sent to his office to be "spanked" with a large wooden paddle.

I was asked to witness such a spanking. The eight-year-old boy, my student, wearing his pants around his ankles, leaned over a chair and staunchly waited for the whoosh of the perforated paddle. It was obviously not his first discipline; his underwear hung loosely over his skinny, black and blue thighs. My heart gasped as the principal continued to whack until tears flowed soundlessly from the child's eyes. Panicking, I fled the room.

I determined to keep my disciplinary issues behind the closed doors of my classroom. One uneventful morning, while walking back to his desk from the pencil sharpener, the same little boy plunged his sharpened pencil into the back of his classmate's hand. I did not want him beaten again. After tending to the slight hand wound, I removed the guilty child to a porch, which faced the rippling creek and a neighboring fish hatchery. As the whine of cicadas blared from the high pines around the porch, the child began to physically tussle with me; I snatched his arm and spun him into a full Nelson. At nine years old, he was as tall as I and much more flexible and stronger. With my legs spread wide to avoid his hearty mule kicks, I whispered loudly into his ear, "I love you and I have ALLLLL day to hold you until you calm down." Forty-five- minutes on the porch evolved into a fond forty-year relationship.

I was often confronted by extreme religiosity, which our parents forced on their children. I noticed a putrid odor emitting from the vicinity of one little girl's desk and traced it to her right ear. She admitted that her ear hurt, and she and her mom had asked God to take the pain away. With my mother-in-law's pressure, her parents finally agreed to take her to a doctor; although, it was too late to save the hearing in that ear.

It was a season of unusual drought. Our crops, trees, and plants needed rain. I turned my Bible time into a time of prayer specifically for rain. I wanted to imprint them with that mustard seed of faith. After all, if the American Indian could bring down rain with a dance, we certainly could with a prayer. As we finished our daily 10-second prayer, we searched the skies, until, after three days of prayer, it began to rain.

Prior to the opening of the school, several of us had donated personal copies of classical children's books, easy-read books, and non-fiction material to fill the empty shelves of the school library. One morning before school, we were alerted of a religious purging prompted by the principal in which the books were being pitched into a metal dumpster and set on fire. Several of us teachers rushed to the smoldering dumpster to retrieve precious literature. Claiming the children needed library skills, a volunteer agreed to sit as a permanent librarian and guard the books.

I floundered in discouragement, ineptness and the inability to create change in the school. I sought out an elder and pleaded with him to DO SOMETHING! I was told to stay in my classroom, love the children, and pray. Which I did.

On a Monday morning, we stood waiting patiently in the school's assembly room for our drill sergeant to open the school day. We were stunned when Sam Fife strode through the double-door entrance, gave us a brief glance, and marched to the front podium to calmly announce that our principal was deceased. (His heart had given out during a furtive alcohol binge.) We watched through our daze as Sam walked from the podium to stand before Miss Mary (teacher, female elder, and mother of three). He raised his hand and placed his palm on her forehead, "You, Mary, are anointed by God to be principal." Then he turned and left the building.

There had been a line of Bowen's Mill principals installed by the ministry after the sergeant died. Out of the seven that I can remember, only two of them had degreed qualifications.

We, the teachers at the school, were not required to prepare lesson plans. Curriculum was inconsistent and outdated. Student files were neglected. The children had no playground and rarely played games. (Sam taught we were to re-create, not recreate the children.) Indiscriminate corporal punishment was administered with a wooden paddle or a leather belt. The school lacked funding and teachers received no compensation. It was chaotic, and the children did not want to be there.

My son, then in elementary, and his cousin were deemed incorrigible and kicked out of the school. I left the school in order to home-school my son and keep up with my farm responsibilities. I did not return to the classroom until after the birth of my third child. During my absence, two male elders, a former butcher and a repairman, became team-principals at the school. Neither men had any educational qualifications, administrative training or experience. They attempted to control the children with stern, insensitive authority to which the students responded with ridicule and lack of respect.

Ryan's older sister, Lynn, and her family considered themselves members of the Move but had not committed themselves to corporate life on a Move farm. They lived in North Carolina where she was a career public school teacher. She was keenly aware and deeply concerned of the state of the Bowen's Mill school and other Move schools. After gaining her father's stamp of approval, she gathered a competent group of teachers from within the Move and initiated a teacher training program. She developed an intense, college-level, six-week course to be given at Bowen's Mill. Participation was mandatory for Bowen's Mill teachers while teachers from other farms were invited to attend.

Commitment and spirituality recognition were gained by living on a Move farm making Lynn's academic credentials secondary to the fact that she did not live in community. Lynn never touted her redeeming position of being Brother Buddy's daughter as she bravely endured the tacit belittlement and scoffing of her "more spiritual" audience.

Her classes exposed our lacks of consistent curriculum, classroom organization, adequate student seating and parent/teacher relationships. I was issued my first lesson plan book with instructions and I was in awe.

The teacher training sessions threw open an essential door for our further enlightenment. The Move had been operating a college in Brussels, Belgium under the direction of an overseas Exxon attorney and his educator wife. To emulate a secondary education, the father ministry had been careful to staff the college faculty with degreed professors and administrators. In 1988, the college, New Covenant Life College, was moved to Alaska with a branch at Bowen's Mill. We also received a proficient elementary educator and degreed administrator who would become our principal. Their assignment was to "straighten out" our degenerating school. They purchased homes at New Covenant and accepted the assignment without salary.

A swing set, merry-go-round and a see-saw appeared in the school yard. We could now teach the children kickball and softball. A ping-pong table was set up in the lunch room for rainy days. Students and teachers donned uniforms, navy blue skirts or slacks for boys with white or baby blue polo shirts, eliminating the disparity between the three-farm dress codes and family income levels. Corporal discipline was rare and only administered by the principal or a parent. The curriculum was organized, books were updated, proper student desks were acquired, heaters and air-conditioners were installed in classrooms. Through donations from the Bowen's Mill congregation, teachers began to receive a small stipend. Children began to look forward to being roused for school.

I was assigned to co-teach under the loving, guiding hand of the former Brussels teacher. She was a degreed, experienced early childhood educator with boundless patience, dry humor and understanding of a six-year-old's mind. We taught first, second and third grades together in one large room, rotating ourselves and the children for each class. She explained her prerequisite for admitting a child to first grade with: "Give me a kindergartner that can flush the toilet, wash his hands and turn out the light and I will teach him how to read."

Our everyday classroom mishaps became entertaining adventures. We saw the gecko that crept his way to the top of the fan grate and slipped, finding himself propelled thru the room like a reptilian cannon ball. A student flushed our classroom commode and misdirected bathroom plumbing flowed hot, steamy water into the bowl. A snake who choose to slumber in a corner under a student's hanging coat was calmly shooed out the door. One horrible morning before the children arrived, we tearfully disposed of a failed incubator science project that produced monstrous chicks with six-inch necks.

The school flourished as the focal point of the three communities. Disagreements between parents and teachers, between a farm and the school, between students and teachers were settled without political drama.

After successfully contributing to the education of one generation of Bowen's Mill students, the principal retired and left Move community. There was no recognition or compensation for her years of service; it was commonly understood that leaving community was never to be cause for celebration.

I left the school to begin a full-time position at Bowen's Mill Convention Center as kitchen manager and secretary of the Board of Directors.

The number of school age children dwindled with the departure of many community residents and little influx of new people. When the last two students reached high school, the school was permanently closed, and the two transferred to a local public high school.

Bowen's Mill School

Bowen's Mill Convention Center is located ten miles north of Fitzgerald, Georgia and is the site of three annual Move conventions, each lasting five days in April, July and

October and one summer youth camp lasting five days in July. The first Bowen's Mill

Convention was held in July 1978 in which attendance swelled to over 1,000 as Moveites from around the globe pitched tents on convention property, filled the two hotels in Fitzgerald or stayed in private homes on the three farms. In later years, urban Move groups built cabins on the grounds for their own convention accommodations. Planning on an apocalyptic event, convention structures were initially built to last seven years. After the seven years passed, buildings were renovated and updated with closed ceilings, indoor plumbing, air-conditioning, and carpeting.

The large pole barn (to be known as the Main Tabernacle) was completed within six weeks with volunteer labor from within the three communities, including two experienced construction foremen. The lumber was milled on-site from trees harvested off the property's 600 acres. With a sawdust floor and open screened sides, the Main Tabernacle had a capacity of 1,500; several meeting rooms, a nursery and a sound booth opened into the meeting area. A handcrafted, wooden pulpit rose from a frontal 8-inch platform on which our traveling and father ministry sat facing the congregation and two smaller platforms held an organ and a Baby Grand out of the sawdust.

The implicit platform seating placed father ministry and notable foreign ministry in the first row of yellow folding chairs with their wives directly behind them on the second row. The remaining three rows were taken by "the rest of the ministry." No one mistook the prime location of Buddy and Dottie's seats. Buddy was immediate stage left of the looming podium with Dottie over his shoulder.

Since convention days counted as Bowen's Mill school days, the meetings were mandatory for school-aged children. From the time they were babies in a port-a-crib until they graduated from high school, my children sat stalwartly through every convention (except to attend young children's Bible classes or to assist in the kitchen).

Their Grandma Dottie situated her seat behind Buddy to have the best view of her grandchildren's goings-on; noting whether they were sleeping, taking notes or fooling around. She counted the times they left the meeting for bathroom breaks and noted with whom they associated. Before the day's end, I received her full report of any objectional behavior with the expectation that I would "do something about it". Sometimes, I did.

Convention meetings, were held twice a day from 9 in the morning until lunch, resuming at 4 P.M. until whenever. Each service opened with a lively, led praise service in which we danced, whooped and hollered, sending the sawdust under our feet into a dense, fibrous fog which clogged our nostrils, tickled our throats and lingered for weeks as sinus congestion.

The first convention kitchen was a screened pole barn with no heat or air conditioning and minimal venting. Cooking was done on scrounged old-timey cast iron stoves or caste-off kitchen stoves. The one walk-in cooler, an old refrigerated truck bed complete with windows, had been dismantled at a Massachusetts farm, trucked to Georgia and reassembled for convention use. We ate from Styrofoam plates, used plastic utensils and drank from Styrofoam cups—all of which were turned back into the kitchen, washed by hand and reused at next meals--until they finally disintegrated.

Three daily meal menus were limited to cheap, farm grown, usually meatless meals of boiled vegetables, rice and hearty, whole wheat bread spread with margarine. Gallon bags of homemade breakfast granola were routinely distributed to those homes that housed convention guests.

The Bowen's Mill convention kitchen ladies were heroes of faith, uncomplaining workers, able to feed the multitudes with little finances and whose only compensation was the joy of service.

I sat through many years of many hours of convention services with my three children until I could bear it no longer. I volunteered to teach a two-hour children's Bible class, which gave me and my children a respite and a snack.

In 1998, I was asked to assume management of the convention kitchen.

Harvesting Pine off Property

Erecting the Main Tabernacle

Main Tabernacle at Bowen's Mill Convention Center 1978

Convention is About to Begin

Not too long ago, I was sitting across from a handsome, attentive man at a swanky restaurant. While blindly gazing into his eyes, my mind stretched beyond the top of his head to the restaurant's bustle of activity. I sensed the kitchen's intense energy as the doors swung open to allow exit and entrance of servers balancing huge trays of plated meals or retrieved empty plates. I am so familiar with the heartbeat of a working kitchen, for it was my heartbeat.

I was in my twenties when I began cooking in the spacious Bowen's Mill Convention Center's kitchen under the apron wings of skilled community cooks. The kitchen had been improved by the donation of two deafening exhaust fans mounted on rolling platforms, which were moved, around the kitchen. The fans blew stable flies out of the kitchen, exhausted the heat, and provided a cooling wind. We still ate the food from Styrofoam plates using plastic cutlery and drank from Styrofoam cups; but we discarded everything after one use.

My first solo kitchen endeavor was a three-farm graduation banquet featuring sliced turkey sandwiches, garnishes, potato salad, and an array of desserts. A day before the May event, I was straddle-legged in front of one of the whirling fans; rivulets of sweat were streaming down my legs; the stench of roasted turkey permeated my clothes and clung to my hair, but--I was having fun! By late afternoon, I was arranging crisp skinned drumsticks and perfectly sliced white meat around four garnished platters. Only the laborious cleanup of greasy pans, utensils and five naked turkey carcasses remained.

Early that morning, I had ridden my bicycle to the Convention Center and planned to end this cook-day with a dip in the coldcold waters of Gar Lake, our favored swimming hole a mile away through dense woods. With the meat in the cooler, the pans scrubbed, and five naked turkey carcasses frozen for soup, I mounted my red Schwinn and pedaled the bumpy, clay road to the river. Behind the veil of drooping cypress trees and Spanish Moss, I stripped off my clothing and dove into the frigid waters. The heat steamed from my body; I lay on my back listening to the chatter of cicadas and relished the rare moment of naked solitude. It was the proper ending to a long, hard cook day.

I acquired full management of the convention kitchen in 1998. The kitchen had finally been fully enclosed and air conditioned; however, the heat from the cast iron ovens often overwhelmed the struggling system.

With the convention kitchen manager's mantle, I also inherited the assistance of Aaron, one of my fifth-grade pupils at our school. Having served time in the kitchen alongside, my formidable predecessor, his grandmother, he knew the convention kitchen better than I and willingly coached me through frequent complications and multiple questions. Though not my last, Aaron was my first "kitchen kid." It was he who set the bar with his impressive work ethic, courteous manner and positive attitude no matter what.

Other amazing young people were added to our convention cook team. Our common goal was to create and serve convention meals that were fabulous, nutritious, pleasingly presented and discouraged conventioneers from going to any restaurant.

Our workday began at 6:30 A.M. with prep and serving of a hot buffet breakfast, continuing into a full-course lunch, supper and a late-night snack or dessert.

Seven to ten volunteer kitchen kids performed two to three hours of prep work per meal consisting of chopping vegetables, tossing salad, baking rolls, portioning dessert and cooking meats. One kitchen kid oversaw the twenty-one volunteer servers who filled plates and passed them through the three serving windows. Two strong, agile kitchen kids were appointed to run food refills and remove empty containers from each station. Unless we were presented with a challenge, we were able to serve the multitudes in less than an hour.

After washing pots and dishes, putting away leftover food, wiping down the serving counters, dumping trash and mopping floors, we closed the kitchen by midnight every night. No kitchen kid shirked responsibility, disappeared from the scene or complained of exhaustion.

Kitchen kids were formally initiated into the permanent convention kitchen crew with the bestowal of a monogrammed apron which was hung proudly on an apron- rack reserved for the kitchen kids. Many of my convention kitchen-kids left Move communities and easily found first jobs with restaurant and service employment.

Convention kitchen exploits were legendary. Often tests of simple faith, they were hilarious at best, momentarily daunting at worst. In every circumstance, somehow, we were miraculously redeemed, and everyone loved us.

Taco salad was our favorite meal to prepare and serve. I did it Taco Bell style: a handful of crushed tortilla chips, hot refried beans, taco-seasoned ground turkey, shredded cheddar cheese, lettuce, chopped tomatoes and salsa. During the serving of a taco salad meal to hundreds, I realized that the cheese was vanishing too quickly. We could NOT run out of shredded cheddar cheese. I grabbed a couple of the convention kitchen kids and we immediately laid hands on the bits of cheese floundering in the bowl and asked God to please multiply the cheese. Inexplicably, I did not have to order shredded cheddar cheese for the next three conventions!

We host an annual five-day Bowen's Mill Youth Camp at the Convention Center during South Georgia's extreme July weather. I had coerced a local watermelon grower to sell us a truckload of watermelon "seconds" for $30.00, delivered. The melons were offloaded into the recycled milk-truck, which served as an unpredictable walk-in cooler.

Every morning, an adult youth-camp volunteer would retrieve ten of the Jubilee watermelons; haul them to the kitchen; cut them into hand-able wedges which were stacked in clean 5-gallon buckets and kept chilled in the cooler. The buckets of crisp, sweet, cold melon were later carried out to playing fields and served to scores of thirsty, sweaty, young campers.

My not-so-secret July kitchen treat was to choose a perfect melon, inject it with vodka and hide it under a shelf in the smaller kitchen walk-in. The kitchen kids knew my secret and knew better than to mess with my melon. On the third afternoon of one camp, I was extremely hot, tired and grumpy, and most annoyed to find my watermelon gone. The missing melon mystery was solved the next day.

I remembered that we had had a novice melon-cutter. When I arrived that morning, he had ten melons rolling precariously on a counter, so I left him to work. Unfortunately, he had found my melon, cut it up and ultimately served the wedges to our unsuspecting teen-aged campers. Thankfully, other than needing a nap, none of the children had gotten ill and my secret was still safe. From then on, my melon wore the Sharpie label: "Miss Cara's. DO NOT TOUCH!"

The Convention Center once leased facilities including three prepared meals per day to ninety-eight AA members on a men's retreat. For their last evening with us, they had requested a celebratory steak banquet. I had purchased one-hundred-twenty-five New York Strips, borrowed a large gas grill from the local bank (Colony Bank in Fitzgerald used to loan cookers) and trained a kitchen kid in the art of grilling steak.

We were ready. The tables were set, iced tea was made and in pitchers, Caesar Salad was fluffed high in bowls and dotted with croutons, baked potatoes sat waiting for butter and sour cream; we heated up the grill. We waited for the grill to heat up. Hungry men began to meander in to the tables, the potatoes were getting chewy in the warming oven and ice was melting in the tea. The grill was not hot. I opened the lid to discover we had been given a smoker rather than a grill! I prayed to get the fast fix; cranked the double-stack convection ovens to 500 degrees; had the kids lay the steaks on full-sized cookie sheets which we slid into the ovens; and blasted them for six minutes before pulling out the sizzling meat. Each steak was tonged and held up while I seared both sides with an acetylene torch. The meal was on time and proved an incredible success!

I certainly never saw myself as perfect. I was capable of screwing-up and the kitchen kids knew it.

During an initial prep for a convention lunch of lemon-pepper tilapia, rice and a salad to serve 650, I instructed one crewmember to pull cases of individually frozen tilapia filets from the walk-in freezer. The fish came flash-frozen, packed in cases of forty individual, quarter-pound fillets. Twelve to

98

thirteen cases of tilapia were required for this meal. Two kitchen kids distributed the fish evenly on lined baking pans, sprayed each portion with olive oil, and, after a dusting of lemon pepper, the pans were shoved into a 350-degree oven for forty-five minutes. The hot pans of baked fish were covered and stacked in bakers' racks while the next round of pans was baking. We needed three rounds of filled pans to feed the crowd. We knew the routine, fulfilled our tasks and were ready to serve.

Well, maybe —

While monitoring the meal's service, I could see that we were rapidly running out of tilapia portions. I told the servers to cut the single 4-ounce pieces of fish in half.

I felt my mouth drying and my neck clenching as I calmly asked, "How many cases of fish did I ask to be pulled from the freezer?" The answer came, "Five."

I shrieked, "FIVE???!!!???"

Sudden brain-drain led to instant-brainstorm. I envisioned small, whole hams on the top shelf of the walk-in waiting to be sliced for the next day's lunch. We jerked them out and sliced quick ham steaks.

As the last parishioner walked away with his full plate, I left the kitchen for a solitary melt-down and pity-party. That one event has remained as my hallmark of failure, a lifetime reminder to consciously consider the immediate details of a job rather than focus on the outcome. Failure is never defeat; failure is the opportunity to do it better next time.

After departing the Bowen's Mill community and my husband, I returned to offer my kitchen assistance for the forthcoming Bowen's Mill Convention. I was told, "It would be better if you did not show up." So, I did not.

Nonetheless, those twelve years were truly some of the best times of my life.

Brother Sam taught that we were not to observe the worldly holidays, not even birthdays. Thus, it was, on all Move farms.

After Sam's death, communities began quietly engaging in holiday celebrations. The July Bowen's Mill Youth Camp and Convention included date of the Fourth of July. We gleefully observed the holiday with fireworks (illegal in our county, but oh, well), sing-a-longs, flash-light tag, roasted hot dogs and s'mores around a massive, roaring bonfire. I hung red-white-and-blue bunting and wore my American flag apron. It was my favorite time of openly and exuberantly celebrating a national holiday.

Halloween, as we were admonished, is the witches' Sabbath. One year, a propagated rumor convinced our community that a local witch coven intended to drive out to Bowen's Mill to harass the Christians. We waited tremulously in prayer that ominous October night, watching the dark starry skies; but nary a witch or goblin appeared, neither did trick-or-treaters.

Thanksgiving was a time of thanking God for our religious freedom. Farm scheduling included preparation of a traditionally huge communal meal. Guests were invited, and fully-costumed children presented entertaining pilgrim and Indian skits. It was fun but, admittedly, I grew to dread the holiday, knowing I would be involved in two days of cooking turkeys and hams followed by a work-intensive clean-up of greasy turkey carcasses, leftover green bean casserole and sticky sweet potatoes. I just wanted to stay home and eat pumpkin pie.

Christmas came and went, for we knew shepherds did not keep their flocks in the field during the winter months, it was just too cold. "Satan Claus" was a propagator of materialism, retail hype and lunacy. There were no letters to Santa, no Christmas trees surrounded by gaily wrapped gifts, no hung stockings, and not even one china nativity scene.

My children and I would drive eight hours south to Mima's house to indulge in her Christmas tree, piles of presents and a grand feast. My children "got to" wear shorts, watch television, swim in the ocean or hang out at her pool. It was a treat that most children in Move communities did not get. I claimed to make the trip to appease my mother, but it was more for my children.

Springtime never brought mention of the giant, candy laden bunny or Easter egg hunts. Easter Sunday always culminated the April Bowen's Mill Convention where it was emphasized that the crucifixion was to be displayed through our "daily dying to self" in hopes of resurrection into immortality.

As years passed, the imposed holiday restrictions gradually eased. The Happy Birthday song was permitted in our dining halls, lighted Christmas trees appeared in living-room windows, Mother's Day corsages were pinned to Sunday best and we had an Easter egg hunt on the Big House lawn.

Holidays became a matter of personal conviction rather than an unequivocal ruling.

Happy Family Times

To drink or not to drink. That was the question.

Having had a European mother, the issue of alcohol consumption in our home was a non-issue. Wine was reserved for mealtimes, conversation times and social times. Liquor was purely social or medicinal. To be drunk was to disgrace oneself; in Mom's opinion a typically crude American habit. My Jewish father would bring home miniature bottles of Manischewitz grape wine (known as children's wine) during holiday times. I was permitted to have a tiny glass of the thick, grapey sweetness after a celebratory meal. I drank hot buttered rum to stay warm, honey and whiskey for a cough, cognac for menstrual cramps and Jager for indigestion.

When I moved into New Covenant, the bottle of wine on the dining room table became the white elephant. I carried my drinks in a Starbucks travel mug; if it was smelled on my breath, then I was standing too close.

There were/are "dry" communities within the Move. Some farms had members sign a pledge never to allow alcohol to touch their lips; some farm left their alcohol edict as "understood"; some farms did not give a flip either way. This promulgation created a wide berth for violation, hypocrisy and justification.

The South Floridians who settled New Covenant were used to a cold beer after mowing grass during sweltering summer days, Margaritas while lounging on a beach and red wine with New York strips seared on a backyard grill. Following the example set by scripture, New Covenant openly allowed wine, but frowned on cold beers and hard liquor (except brandy in Christmas eggnog or poured, flaming, over Baked Alaska). New Covenant was the only one of the three Bowen's Mill communities to admittedly engage in the drinking of alcohol earning us the title of "Carnal Covenant."

My husband and I visited a community in Great Britain which strictly forbade the consumption of any form of alcoholic beverage. While peeling potatoes on kitchen duty, I happened upon a healthy cache of various liquors and wines perched unobtrusively on a low kitchen pantry shelf. I exclaimed, "Oh, my! What do we have here?" and questioned a staunch English elder about the clandestine stash, to which he replied, "Those bottles are purely for medicinal purposes." My subsequent groans of a bellyache, a sore toe, and a scratchy throat were totally ignored.

While washing dishes on a dry community hidden within the Northern wildernesses of Alaska, I discovered a wine cache hidden among bottles of cleaning supplies under the wash sink. I confronted the nearest elder who maintained, "No one drinks here."

As generations passed through Move communities, drinking habits became less of an issue. After all, Jesus was called a "winebibber" and He made it just fine.

After an early childhood in the Bronx, my dad's military career took our family from Governor's Island to Japan and beyond. My native Hungarian mother coached us through every new country's culture; we ate the food, we learned the languages, we sang the songs, we partied with the natives. I yielded to her liberal training but strained against her strict maternal boundaries.

My mother was not a church-going woman, but she was an open-minded woman who believed in telepathic communication and a spiritual realm. She shared her beliefs with her children and taught us awareness of things unseen. She maintained that if she were able, after death, she would return to me.

It was easy for me to accept spirituality as taught by the Move. Deliverance from demons was sensible.

Deliverance services went beyond any sensibility.

I had first heard of Jane's deliverance from a taped session produced by a university study, which confirmed the reality of her exorcism performed by Sam Fife. (http://zionstrumpet.org/Deliverance.htm)

I did not meet Jane Miller until years after her spiritual liberation and was instantly allured by her vibrant energy, sparkling eyes, tight hugs and high spikey heels. She and her husband became family favorites as they lovingly nurtured a close relationship with us and our three children. They became "anointed" leaders of an itinerant "deliverance team" who, upon request, performed mass, public exorcisms in Move communities and urban Move fellowships.

The Bowen's Mill eldership decided to invite the team to deliver our three-farm population from any indwelling, unwelcome demon spirits. Our school and each farm were directed to adjust routine daily scheduling to accommodate the times of deliverance services, which extended from early morning to late night, 24/7, and, thankfully, included mealtime breaks. It was decided to hold the services in our spacious New Covenant tabernacle.

Our nearby homes were made available as nurseries, playrooms, and snack stations for younger children. Deliverance days were designated as school days, making the attendance at deliverance services mandatory for all school-aged children.

Three high stools were placed in the center of the vast dining hall, red metal chairs sat folded against one perimeter wall, an upright piano and a gleaming drum set dominated a designated praise area near the entrance and full boxes of tissues were placed conveniently under each stool.

By 8:30 each morning, the three-farm congregation began to arrive as musicians set up instruments, women arranged pitchers of ice water and clean glasses in the kitchen while the deliverance team prepared for spiritual battle. Prophets, pen and paper in hand, stood close to the scene of action, ready to record and report any visions or spiritual messages.

As I entered the tabernacle, I heard the growing cacophony of conversation, tuning instruments and frolicking children and thought, "This is like a three-ring circus! All we lack is elephants, clowns, and cotton candy."

The increasing crowd evolved into a large circle encompassing the three empty stools. Instrumental music and the clanging of tambourines filled the room as voices rose harmoniously in robust songs of praise to God and victory over Satan. As each of the three stools became occupied by a willing member of the congregation, we, who stood in the wide circle, began to clap and dance vigorously as we paraded around the three stooled subjects.

Deliverance service had officially begun.

An absolute deliverance from demonic presence was punctuated by loud shouts of "Amen!" and "Hallelujah!" as the deliverer prompted the delivered to raise his/her arms in gratitude. As each victorious, freed subject stood, the stool was instantly relinquished to the next demonized victim.

There were times when indwelling demons were excessively rambunctious and obstinately reluctant to relinquish their stronghold on the one in the chair.

A lovely, quiet, reserved woman, who had once been a classical ballerina, sat solemnly atop the middle stool. Her deliverer gently placed hands on her shoulders, closed her eyes, and began to pray, commanding demons to leave the usually tranquil woman. It was as though a vicious banshee had suddenly jumped on the stool, for the woman began to spit, hiss and curse like an angry bar whore. We, as bystanders, had previously been instructed not to react to whatever activity might occur on the stool. However, this activity was overwhelming. My immediate reaction was provoked by the shared reaction of her two pre-teen children who stood near their venom spouting mother; their mouths agape, transfixed by their mother's shocking transformation. I grabbed their hands, forcibly ushering them through the clamorous crowd and out the door and dragged them across the yard to my mobile home for distractive cookies and cocoa. Repercussive gossip eventually prompted the family to leave community and adopt a more reclusive lifestyle.

During one evening service, two female social workers from town unwittingly, unexpectedly appeared to witness the turbulent deliverance of a colossal man who suffered from grand mal epileptic seizures. His thunderous cries overrode the music as he thrashed, yelled and swung at his deliverer from his seated position. Men were beckoned to assist in carefully lying the man on the carpeted floor where he continued to harmlessly kick and holler. The two women had joined the New Orleans style march circling the three stools, while daintily hopping over the man's protruding size fourteen feet. They appeared to be blinded, oblivious to his exuberant performance and left without comment. His deliverance remained legendary as did his continued seizures.

My younger daughter's constant companion, a towheaded young neighbor boy, suffered from viral warts infesting both his eyelids. The five-year-old boy climbed nervously onto the stool. His deliverer closed her eyes, laid her hands gently over his eyes and began to quietly pray. That night he went to bed with the warts but awoke the next morning without warts. He has remained miraculously wart-free.

I took my turn on the stool. My deliverer stroked my head as she parted my hair from my ear and whispered words of encouragement. "Relax. Think about the Lord. Open your mouth and speak in tongues. Do you have anything you want to tell me?" I thought I did and readily revealed childhood abuse and pain. Her grip tightened on my shoulder as she placed her other palm tightly against my forehead, her steely voice proclaiming, "In the name of Jesus, demon come out! Cara is covered by the blood of Jesus! You have no dominion here! Leave!"

When it was over, I did not feel any differently leaving the chair than when I first took the chair. I did simultaneously stop biting my nails.

The three Bowen's Mill communities appeared to be infested with legions of demons as deliverance services continued non-stop, every day, for weeks without interruption. Everyone (nearly 200 of us) had demons lurking within. Well, almost everyone.

The deliverance team determined that two of our men were demon-free. My father-in-law----and his son, my husband.

The deliverance team left us exhausted, satisfied and demonless. They became Move celebrities, traveling to farms and city groups nationwide until all had been given the opportunity for deliverance from demon spirits.

It really happened. I remember it well.

I Danced at Deliverance

Communal living presented ample opportunities for disagreement, misunderstanding, miscommunication and intense squabbling. A Biblical foot-washing ceremony was a way of humbling oneself, burying the hatchet and resuming the relationship. The New Covenant family participated in the infrequent event, one of the rare occasions for which I scrubbed my soles and painted my toes.

We each came wearing slip-off shoes and carrying a Bible and a clean, unstained towel. My linen closet held towels reserved for foot-washing for I certainly did not want to unfold a ratty-tatty towel in front of my neighbors.

As I entered the Tabernacle, I geared myself up for the emotional scenario of kneeling before someone and washing their feet. Worse still, was to have someone kneel in front of me and wash my feet! It was an uncomfortably intimate experience.

A hushed, reverent aura floated around us, as we all chose seats from the last two rows of cushioned chairs. The first two rows were arranged with berth for a kneeler and a white Rubbermaid dishpan. A curly-locked lass played soft praise music on the Baldwin upright; I sat waiting, staring at my hands resting on my Bible and towel in my lap and relaxed into the soothing melodies.

113

A farm elder stood up behind the wide wooden pulpit to begin the service with a recitation of the Biblical narrative depicting the first foot washing. (John 13:1-17) The piano played on as we began to rise, towel in hands, from our seats to occupy a tub-flanked chair.

I preferred to be a first participant; "get it done" is my motto. I rose, placed my Bible on my red cushioned chair and took a seat in the front row.

A male elder carried a 5-gallon bucket from the mop sink and poured tepid water into my white Rubbermaid dishpan. I placed my lime green Crocs under my seat, slid my feet into the warm water, closed my eyes, sniffed the bleachy smell from my towel and waited.

I felt a light splash of water against my ankles. I squinted to see the outline of a bouffant hairdo kneeling before me. I leaned over to place my hand lightly on poofyness to demonstrate my acceptance of her humility. My inside thoughts were, "Please get done, please get done, please hurry." She gently dried my cleansed tootsies, we exchanged smiles, hugged over the dishpan and changed positions.

My neighbor had chosen to wear nylons. Why would anyone wear nylons to a foot-washing? There was a distinct creepy feel to washing stockinged feet besides that they were sopping, dripping wet when raised from the tub. My clean towel was now soaked.

We shared soulful looks and a deep hug before returning to our Bibles.

A communion service followed the foot-washing ceremony.

Our moderating elder led us into a wide, hand-clasped circle. Hands joined or not, we dropped our heads in an attitude of prayer as we listened to the retelling of the Last Supper. Four elders carried trays of grape-juice-filled 1-once cups and bits of broken matzo. We did use Mogen David until the kids wandered innocently to the kitchen, assumedly to get a drink. It was a drink all right, they drank the un-drunk wine. It was grape juice from then on.

One of the children refused to participate in the communion service. She claimed it was "gross" to be drinking Jesus' blood and pretending like we were eating his body!

I had never thought of it from that angle.

Sam Fife promoted the religious opinion that to own a pet prompted inordinate affection between man and beast. To gain admittance to any Move farm, one had to leave all pets behind, including service animals.

I had a youthful ambition to become a veterinarian which filled my childhood with assorted pets. The first was a Boston Bull Terrier named Jingles who raced up and down the long hallway of our two-bedroom Bronx apartment. Jingles had an infatuation with my baby brother's toes and, at every opportunity, he nibbled them. Jingles was given away.

When I was five, my father brought home a fluffy, brown hamster in a small cage with a running wheel. I was told never to open the cage, for fear he would escape into the hidden recesses of my bedroom. I was permitted to stick a pencil thru the bars to pet my hamster with the eraser end. When I inserted my index finger for an illegal stroke, the hamster bit the tip of my finger off.

While we lived in military housing in Japan, my dad surprised me with three downy, yellow Easter chicks who quickly grew into three young rambunctious roosters. My mother, the animal lover, penned them with plywood in a narrow space between her kitchen stove and a wall. Their cracklings and crowing's entertained her until they became spry enough to leap over their barricade and steal food from the counters.

To meet my need of caring for a pet, my parents gave me Duke, a gentle, brindle boxer. I became obsessed with his training and entered him a in a JKC (Japan Kennel Club) obedience show. After our proud prance around the ring, with their heads bouncing, the judges whispered rapidly in Japanese and beckoned to my beaming father; I became highly excited thinking we had won first place! Not to be....my dog was disqualified for having only one testicle. From then on, my mother called him "Duke, The One-Balled Wonder."

There were other pets, other inordinate affections for my animals. Knowing pets were forbidden on the farms, I did my best to avoid cuddly puppies, cute kittens and soft bunnies. However, in quiet defiance of the "no pet" rule, New Covenant residents kept silent goldfish or claimed legitimate contributing farm critters, ducks, chickens, goats or calves.

And so, it was until field mice invaded the camp and left their droppings in kitchen drawers and shredded towels in bathroom cupboards. The elders decided to permit each household one outside cat. During my three decades of community living, I owned three cats: a huge yellow tabby named Lyin' King, an aggressive Manx who disappeared and Maverick, who retired with me in Florida and was killed by a wandering bobcat.

Dogs were prohibited until we thought we needed a herd dog for the cattle. Inky, a black Border

Collie, joined New Covenant and took up residence under our trailer.

Despite all our good intentions, the only moving object Inky herded was the mailman's delivery truck.

Inky did enjoy our morning runs and would bound exuberantly into the woods to chase fleeting deer or to tree a bewildered racoon. One day, after a hard rain turned the back road into a muddy mess, I ran the highway with Inky happily exploring alongside. He made the mistake of leaping into the road to chase a log-loaded semi. To my horror, he glanced off a rear tire, flew spinning into the air and tumbled into the grass where he lay too still. I knew he was dead. I turned and raced home, sobbing, to rouse my husband from bed. As I stumbled into our driveway, blinded by tears and heaving for breath, Inky limped from under our mobile home. He had survived to beat me home! Years later, he passed away unceremoniously while napping on the tabernacle porch.

Locals often dropped off their unwanted animals near the farm's red-brick entryway, believing that we, the church, would surely give them a good, long life. We did not, they were euthanized country style with a shotgun.

As Move mandates usually do, the "no pet" rule eventually slipped away leaving the community with too many dogs and a score of feral cats. I had learned Sam's lesson well and did not allow myself to bond with any animal until I left New Covenant.

I acquired Sammy, a black Golden Doodle. My affections for him poured out unrestrained by doctrine or opinion. He lived for only two years before being taken by a deadly disease. My initial thoughts on his passing was that God had taken Sammy because of my inordinate affection for him.

It was a deep indoctrination.

July 1979 marked the start of the second Bowen's Mill Convention series. Ryan was standing on the ministry platform before the entire congregation to be set-in as an elder. Existing elders nominate those who demonstrate an anointing by God to lead, serve and govern non-elders who live together on Move farms or co-exist in city groups or "bodies." Elder candidates who exhibit consistent exemplary spiritual performance for one year are presented to the traveling ministry for approval. Called to the platform during public sessions, each nominee stands midst the ministry who place their hands somewhere on his/her body, pray aloud, speak in tongues or prophecy and set him/her into his new role as a functioning elder.

Elders govern, counsel, make community decisions and are involved in the personal lives of church members. Elders attend many elders' meetings. If one in a marriage is an elder and the spouse is not, the non-elder is excluded from all elder activities. I was happy to remain a non-elder and watched as my husband gradually floated away from me on the sacred mantle of his elite position.

My son was attending first grade in a cold, cramped, stone out-building on the edge of Highway 129 near House Creek Bridge. Jason and his four classmates sat on wooden chairs at a shared table monitored by a stern, grey-haired teacher who whacked their palms with a wooden ruler at the slight infraction of dropping their hands to their laps. They were required to leave their shoes at the door and were forbidden to participate in recess until they could tie their own shoelaces. I purchased Velcro sneakers.

Across the road in a 12 x 12 room with a window view of piney woods, I was teaching three grades of eight elementary children. My curly headed, dimpled second-grader approached my desk to place a small pink, beaded coin purse next to my hand. "Miss Cara," she lisped, "this is for your new baby girl." "Why, Sharon, I am not having a baby. I am not pregnant." "Yes, you are," she asserted.

Turned out, I was pregnant. My husband groaned, "How did that happen?" A friend suggested I name the baby "Manna," meaning "what is this?"

I wanted a home birth. The Move has its own midwifery force, trained by ladies who had been licensed midwives. None of the midwives were licensed in Georgia, thus home deliveries attended by an unlicensed midwife were illegal for us in the Bowen's Mill communities unless the father caught the newborn at birth.

We believed God's direction superseded the law of the land.

I awaited our second child in our upstairs bedroom while I viewed the rest of the farm harvesting November pecans in the orchard bordering the Big House yard. During the last term of pregnancy, I had been excused from scrambling on my knees through dry leaves and cow paddies in the search for brown pecan nuggets.

My midwife, a formerly licensed missionary midwife, had been living with us for weeks and had already sanitized and re-sanitized our bedroom several times, hoping to prompt my delayed labor through covert coercion. She had a dated plane ticket to fly home after the delivery and it would have cost her to change the ticket for which we would have had to pay. I was two weeks past due and totally ready to have the baby.

The fervent prayers of righteous men were obviously successful as labor began on a Tuesday night while a prayer meeting occurred in the living room downstairs. I had developed a pounding headache for which I took a Tylenol, effectively interrupting the birthing process for exactly four hours. Labor resumed with fierce contractions, pushing my lovely, chocolate brown-eyed daughter into the world within minutes. She lay quietly on my chest, pushed up with her downy arms to serenely survey her new surroundings and smiled.

The midwife left my baby and me confined to our tower bedroom for a week during which we were entertained by steady stream of baby admirers.

I was delighted by a visit from Herbert Player. Herbert was a tall, regal man with deep dark eyes set in a noble profile. His coffee skinned arms were protected by starched, French-cuffed dress shirts buttoned to his neck and tucked into pressed trousers.

He lived in a pristine white cottage hidden deep within dark cypress woods adjoining our sugar cane mill. Carved crosses graced white shutters framing each of his eight windows and a freshly whitewashed picket fence encompassed his manicured yard.

Herbert owned no car, no tractor, no power tools, no gas mower. He planted and harvested his bountiful vegetable garden by moon cycles. He raised a yearly pig and calmly bumped it on its head with a sledgehammer while its snout was buried in a bucket of meal, after which he hung it on low tree limbs by its back hooves and slit its throat.

Herbert accurately forecast the weather by examining the bend of tree leaves; they reach high to catch raindrops and droop low to rest in the sun. He picked corn when the tassels were black and cut okra early in the morning when the green pods held full flavor. He loved God and never lied. Locals called him an eccentric old hermit, I knew he was a genius.

At age 80, Herbert married the love of his life, Mary, age 70. He said he robbed the cradle. Mary lived in the town of Fitzgerald and continued to do so. She drove her aged Ford down the dusty clay roads to visit her Herbert in the morning and performed wifely chores before enjoying a quiet dinner with her beloved. Mary returned to town in the dusk of evening to do it over again the next day.

Despite his adoration for Mary, Herbert confessed that he could never live in a busy city like Fitzgerald. On cold, lonely winter nights, he lay back in his worn, leather recliner, with his nightly cigarette in hand and his filled whiskey glass on a near side table. His one propane heater toasted his toes and warmed his house.

The morning Herbert came to meet our baby, he refused to climb the stairs to our bedroom. He said he had never been in the bedroom of a white woman and never would be. My husband carried our baby down the stairs and placed her in Herbert's strong, gentle arms.

On a Sunday before church, Herbert's distraught nephew banged on our back-porch door. He had been to pay his weekly respects to his legendary uncle and discovered the tidy clapboard cottage burned to the ground.

My husband found Herbert's charred skull and breastbone under a melted panel of French doors. Slumbering soundly in his recliner, he had forgotten a teapot left whistling on his stove. It had ignited, shooting flames through the gas line to burst from his one propane heater.

My infant daughter was six weeks old when my husband received a message from God that he was to accompany an elderly minister on a tour, extending from Georgia north to Canada and Alaska, stopping to preach at several of the Move wilderness farms en route. To amuse myself during his absence, I cut a pattern from a brown paper bag and fashioned a pair of cozy size 12 slippers from sheepskin scraps sent to me from a Northern farm. The handsewn slippers were finished in time for his return two months later.

Three years slipped by before I became unexpectedly pregnant with our third child. Once again, my husband's initial comment was, "How did that happen?" My mother-in-law slammed her fist on a table and asked me if I expected she and Buddy to continue supporting our growing family. I had no answer for her, for Buddy consistently maintained that God had directed him to carry our finances if Ryan stayed on the farm. Apparently, Buddy had not shared his divine communication with his wife.

Since we needed more than our two upstairs bedrooms, we were moved from the Big House to the Little House, a three-bedroom bungalow situated on a grassy lot shaded by an ancient pecan tree behind the Big House.

I continued my work schedule at the Big House, carried my load of farm chores and finished teaching through that school term. The pregnancy crawled through the short, Georgia winter into the long sultry days of summer. Other than cooking and cleaning, my beach ball belly exempted me from the grueling summer schedule.

A close friend, Juliette, had enrolled in the Move's midwifery training. With my experienced midwife in attendance, my second home delivery was to be Juliette's first practical performance. We were both very, very excited.

My bourgeois European mother had been sedated during her own deliveries and desired to witness this birth of her grandchild. I was wary because she had not supported my previous home delivery and had threatened to kill my husband if any disaster befell me. I fully believed her. At seventy-three, she was a full-time Holiday Inn office manager and planned her vacation to coincide with my due date. I never reminded her how late my second baby had been and was confident that I would be spared her opinionated presence at this baby's birth.

I was wrong.

It was a Friday yard-house cleaning day for everyone at the Big House. Juliette, Dottie, Rose and my mother were raking flower beds and pulling weeds. I was baking corndogs in air-conditioned comfort in Dottie's kitchen. Ryan was completing an electrical project in the pump house. The first burst of labor hit me as the corn dogs slid into the oven. I summoned my midwife, who deduced that it was probably initial contractions or, perhaps, Braxton Hicks. Nevertheless, she took over lunch prep as I stumbled out the back door to our house and my bed.

The midwife sent my husband to check on me; I told him that I felt the baby crowning. He did not believe me, and returned to his tasks after summoning Juliette, who, upon examination of my cervix, confirmed my perception.

Suddenly, our cozy little home bustled with activity as the set changed to a birthing room.

I had delivered baby #2 while reclining on a six-foot table borrowed from the dining hall. It had not proven a comfortable experience, so, for this delivery, I had requested additional back support. My husband had designed a custom birthing chair resembling something out of an old horror movie; a cushioned wooden-recliner perched atop concrete blocks complete with wood-framed birthing-stirrups.

My mother stood by my left side, my mother-in-law close, ready to remove my mom from the room if necessary. My husband and Juliette stood at my feet, arms flexed, to receive the baby. The midwife coached us into the ensuing operation.

Things changed quickly. I was firmly commanded to cease from the final thrusts of labor. Shoving aside my husband and Juliette, the midwife silently moved into position between my trembling legs. I was not told that three loops of the umbilical cord were tightly wrapped around the baby's neck. The midwife slipped her hand into the birth canal and deftly manipulated the baby's head while she slid a scalpel against her neck and severed the cord. My newborn daughter slithered into her hands and I could see that she was a deep, dark, quiet, motionless purple.

The world became slow motion. I envisioned liquid plastic pouring from a vessel over my mother's head encasing her soundlessly in a plexiglass box. I heard everyone pull in their breath. I saw the midwife stick a tube down my baby's throat and rhythmically begin to gently suck and blow. Within extremely long seconds, my daughter sputtered and bleated.

We cheered and thanked God.

I still tease Juliette about being my only girlfriend to have had her hand in my vagina.

My mother remembered the delivery as being emotional, short and the most beautiful event she had ever experienced.

I never contradicted her.

Herbert and Mary's Wedding

On a lazy fall afternoon, my younger daughter, then a toddler, was playing in our yard under the wide limbs of the ancient oak named "Bull Tree." The fence line had once enclosed Bull Tree into the cow pasture where its cool shade was the favorite napping spot for our herd of Brangus cows and one ornery bull named Ferdinand. Although there was never a near confrontation, my children never trusted Ferdinand to stay within his confines. As we passed the leisurely ruminating herd while on our daily strolls, we were guaranteed safe passage by bravely singing our cow song: "Moooooove cows, don't bother me. Moooooove cows, don't bother me."

To accommodate the placement of our mobile home, the fence line was moved, the cows relocated, and Bull Tree became the climbing tower, rope swing tether and shady protector of frolicking children.

I was inside cleaning the refrigerator while a neighbor teen kept a watchful eye on young children playing in our yard. The kitchen wall phone rang. I tucked it under my chin as I dragged the long cord to finish scrubbing dried, spilled milk from a glass shelf. Thru my free ear, I heard a sharp outcry, "Miss Cara, SNAKE!"

Snake sightings were common. Egg stuffed rat snakes slumbered under warm bellied hens; coral snakes twined through woodpiles and gargantuan timber rattlers spanned across local roadways.

The phone clattered to the floor as I swung open the porch door and caught sight of a lengthy rattlesnake lazily stretched in the shadow of my rosemary bush. Rattlesnakes gorge themselves before bedding down and sharing a gopher tortoise den for the winter. Rattlesnakes must coil before striking, and this snake had no intention of coiling; thankfully, he was just too fat, full and sleepy.

The trembling teen stood under Bull Tree, her eyes as big as fried eggs. To the left of the motionless snake stood my toddler in pink flip-flops, bent inches from the snake's raised head and flickering tongue, peering intently into his eyes. I spoke in a low, controlled monotone, "Angela, I want you to quickly and carefully step back two steps. Then I want you to make a big circle around Mr. Snake and come here to me on the porch. Now!"

"But, Mom, I am looking at his eyes to see if he is a good snake."

I taught the children how to identify venomous pit vipers. Round-eyed snakes are good snakes; slanty-eyed snakes are bad snakes.

Nevertheless, Angela obeyed and taking her own way, she stepped daintily on the snake's head as she hopped on the porch beside me. I sent the other children home. The snake remained nonplussed, unmoving in the hope that no one had really discovered him.

I retrieved a hard rake and square shovel from the backyard shed and, thus armed, approached the rattle-end of the still snake. Lifting the rake with my left hand, I thrust it high on his body to secure him while quickly severing his head off with the shovel's sharp edge. His mouth gaped, the venomous fangs viciously protruded from his fading pink gums. His headless, bleeding body continued to sway from the teeth of the rake. I left him to death and dug a hole on the other side of the fence.

I showered and prepared my three children for the daily corporate supper.

The children urged me to share the snake story with the farm family after dinner. I did, ending with a burst of tears at the realization of what could have been.

Sometimes things happen in our day-to-day life, which are quick, fleeting moments of spirit intervention, occurrences which have no other explanation other than miraculous. We are often unaware of their importance unless it involves life or death situations.

In 1971, the Hollywood congregation of the Move unanimously elected to establish their own school. Parent-teachers were selected and trained by two certified teachers who would function as our school administrators. The elders decided that my expired Red Cross Water Safety Instructor certification and my love for children qualified me as an elementary teacher teaching first and second grades.

The fledgling school leased a church building in North Miami with a wide playing field and monkey bars. We thought our school had found its forever home. It was not to be. After draining the church's bank account, the good-looking pastor left his wife to elope with his secretary to some faraway paradise. We lost the lease and searched for another building. For the remainder of that first year, we teachers became itinerate teachers traveling to homes in Broward and North Dade.

I was uncomfortably pregnant with my first child and my clothing stuck to my sweaty belly as I drove from house to house, getting out and into the car, schelpping piles of books and supplies. I felt like an intruder, often witnessing the struggles as families adjusted to having their children schooled at home by church friends. I found it difficult to have parents inject their control and discipline while I attempted to teach their child. Even the pets were stressed. Before allowing me entry into his house, an eye-level Doberman clicked his jaw before nearly snapping the nose off my face.

Eventually, another North Miami church opened its doors to our school. I was asked to assist carpooling Broward County students to the new location, a forty-five-minute drive each way. I was permitted to bring my Afghan Hound, Hussan, to school where he busied the day away under my desk and happily joined the children in recess play. By this time, though resembling the little, tipping teapot, I continued to teach through the term.

I carpooled while driving a 1970 VW Fastback (stick shift, light beige exterior, tan leather interior) which we had purchased new for $1,500 from the VW factory in Wolfsburg, Germany. The U.S. government had graciously transported the car from Bremerhaven to New York City, where we picked it up to drive to Florida. My husband of six months had quietly mapped out a surprise honeymoon side-trip to the Rocky Mountains. A day after leaving the Big Apple, we arrived in Rocky Mount — a small town in Tennessee with nary a hill in sight. An old man rocking on a gas station porch nearly popped his suspenders as I leaned out the window hollering,

"Could you please tell me where the mountains are?" It became a standing joke in our marriage.

My first carpool pick-up was Marsha in Hollywood; Marsha was the adopted, indulged, over-spanked six-year-old daughter of elderly Move parents. Two sisters, Joni and Ester, joined us in Hallandale; although, a year apart, the two girls were often mistaken for identical twins. My three passengers shared the rear seat; Hussan rode shotgun with his long snout stuck out the window and his golden-haired ears flapping in the wind.

That afternoon, Marsha had to be dropped off first to meet a dance class. I had watched her go thru the front door before driving the squabbling sisters south to their mobile home in a trailer park behind the Coca Cola plant. I pulled up to a stop sign on 58th and Johnson Street, the first busy intersection north of the Hollywood Fashion Square. I could hear the girls giggling as I looked both ways before easing across the well-traveled, two-lane road through town. Instantly, an unseen force wretched the steering wheel from my grip and spun my car into a hard-left turn. In a slow-motion moment, we floated from the turn to a jolting stop with the engine still running. I had eased directly into the path of an eastbound heavy, black dump truck and had been hit broadside on Hussan's side.

One of the sisters flung open her passenger door to bolt to my side. Eyes wide with terror, she flung open my door and asked, "Miss Cara, are you okay?" Though dazed, I was fine, as was Hussan and her sister behind me. My Wolfsburg pride resembled a crippled crab, but we were fine.

In later years, I would often revisit that intersection and sit at the same stop sign, wondering, "How did I not see that truck!"

Over the next twenty years, I was involved in thirteen automobile accidents of which two were my fault.

The last, in 1983, was the worst.

I was driving my Dodge Caravan to town with four children, including one in an infant seat. It was to be a routine errand day to end with milk shakes at Sonic. My ten-year old son, Jason, and six-year old daughter, Louise, sat in back, counting pennies from a chipped Mason jar, hoping they had enough for nonessential purchases.

Ten miles south of Bowen's Mill, Otter Creek Bridge crosses Highway 129. Flanking the narrow, two-lane overpass at the bottom of a blind hill was Easy Harper's, a beer, milk and cigarette stop. As I breached the top of the hill, I could see a semi-truck pulling half of a northbound doublewide trailer rapidly approaching giving slim chance for both our vehicles to simultaneously cross the bridge. Instinctively, my foot eased on the brakes to slow our speed -- shrill screams suddenly burst from the back seat.

I turned my head as my son hurled himself forward over the middle seats into the backside of the passenger seat landing with a quiet thud against the sliding side door.

A violent rear impact propelled our van forward into a slight right turn to a grassy swale just before the bridge. Not wearing a seatbelt, I tucked my legs tightly under my seat and locked my grip on the steering wheel and told God that I was not going to abandon the children by flying through the windshield. Our van came to an abrupt stop, engine still running. The semi and trailer had continued northward. We were parked in high, soft grass; behind us, a fully loaded logging truck was stopped in middle of the road. The driver jumped from his cab and was running toward us, yelling.

My son lay on the floor, his head bleeding from several superficial wounds. The baby and the child next to her were seemingly unaware of what happened. Louise sat, stunned on her seat, glistening glass fragments from the rear windshield illuminating her hair like a Christmas angel. The driver's seat had buckled, trapping me against the steering wheel.

I yelled at my son, "Jason!!!" His groggy response quickly turned to hysteria as he attempted to climb over me to get to the truck which he had seen hit us. "I'm going to get you!" he screamed, "My daddy's gonna beat you up!" In the attempt to calm him, I had no choice but to slap his cheek to inhibit his dive at the truck driver who was at my window crying, "Oh, my god! Oh, my god! I did not realize there were children in here! Oh, my god!" He fled up a hill to Easy Harper's and a phone (pre-cellphone days). I managed to extract myself and tend to the children, who, though shaken, were unharmed.

The uninsured, fully-loaded logging truck with faulty brakes and balding tires had been barreling behind us. His vehicle had just topped the hill as he saw my brake lights flash at the bottom of the hill. The driver confessed to me that not being able to control his speed and not wanting to flip his load, he had decided to hit us. It was not the truck's first accident.

Two neighbors from the farm drove by on their way to town. Seeing us parked in the grass, they both stopped to help; one offering to take Louise and the fourth child with her to the library; the other transported Jason, me and the baby to the hospital for assessment of Jason's head lacerations.

My husband had been home at New Covenant loading a huge boar onto a trailer for a day at the hog auction. I managed to contact him from the emergency room. Within a short time, he pulled into the emergency room parking area with the snorting hog pushing against the trailer's gate. I encouraged him to proceed to the auction, which he did.

The doctor cleaned Jason's wounds and suggested that we seek a chiropractic analysis of my son's back. Our old, country chiropractor took x-rays of Jason's spine and back, and with a smirk, gave his professional diagnosis. "Mrs. Cobb, your son's back looks fine. All healthy. Except for this key." A key? Embedded in his back? What key? Holding the x-ray against a light, his index finger pointed to a key, clearly visible to the lower left of my son's spine.

I looked questioningly at Jason as his face flushed and his eyelids began to flutter. "Okay, so what is with that key? I demanded, my voice rising.

"Umm, Mom, it is the key to Granddad's gun case in my back pocket."

"Does your granddad know you have the key to his gun case?"

"No."

The police report stated that I had completely stopped the van on the highway, blocking the bridge for the logger. Logging is a very important to the economy of South Georgia and logging trucks possess police immunity. We chose not to pursue a lawsuit and settled for a new van.

I have often wondered if that entire accident was orchestrated to uncover the nicked gun case key.

The first deliverance farm was a remote, grassy field in Homestead, Florida. The mission was to free those who were "bound" by demonic activity demonstrated through evil thoughts or deeds. Comprised of one mobile home, the deliverance work was initially performed by a couple who began taking in incorrigible young women; removing outside influences and hoping for the best by loading up on Bible teaching, assigning daily chores, tough love and praying out demons. The number of deliverees of increased rapidly, forcing them to seek other property and additional help. They moved the entire work to Mississippi and eventually, in 1977, to Georgia where the deliverance community or farm became known as the Ridge.

Deliverance work is not for the faint hearted or the thin skinned. The Ridge, and other deliverance farms, are populated by drug addicts, mentally afflicted, physically disabled, emotionally disturbed…the blind, lame and halt seeking help and those who felt the calling to care for them. All come without debt, without job ties, without outside influence. Residents sign a vow to abstain from alcohol and to agree to the Godly mandates imposed upon them by the farm government, the elders.

It is said that all residents are there for deliverance.

The caregivers, or ministry, often live with their assigned charges, 24/7. Where one is, the other is, also. A single man may be in the care of another single man—together they would work, shave, eat and sleep. A young woman escaping drugs and boyfriends might have to sleep protected by her female counterpart.

Dali, my close girlfriend, lived down the road from us at the Ridge. Dali had blundered into community accompanying a boyfriend. After several good meals and clean, comfy beds, boyfriend left, and Dali stayed. Anton had been a revolutionary of sorts who had stumbled into the Move thru a traveling ministry. He immigrated to the States, committed himself to the deliverance ministry and met Dali. They walked out their year of courtship, married and lived their life amidst the physically and mentally challenged.

Despite having suffered several miscarriages, Dali and Anton were blessed with two beautiful daughters. When Dali found herself pregnant once again, she was determined to carry the baby to full term. She also wanted a midwife attended home birth in her aluminum mobile home at the Ridge.

Dali and her husband had requested the elders' blessing for their home birth. In Dali's case, despite her prenatal history, the eldership felt it would be God's will for her to deliver her baby at home......in a built-on foyer to their trailer, with a Move midwife and me as the midwife's immediate assistant. Although, the midwife had been a registered nurse and licensed midwife, my qualifications were my own home births and attendance at several others.

When the time arrived... I was summoned and quickly took a disinfectant shower and changed into sanitized, loose clothing. I drove the two miles to find Dali's home a flurry of activity. Her young daughters had been sent to a neighbor. The home reeked of Betadine; crisp, oven-sterilized sheets draped the birthing bed; a pot of clean water sat simmering on the stove. Dali lay sprawled on her bed, her legs dangling near the bottom edge of the plastic-covered mattress, writhing in the piercing pain of back labor.

My position was to be kneeling on the floor between Dali's legs, keeping her clean and comfortable with a pan of warm water and soft towels. The midwife stood over me directing the progression of labor. Dali's husband was at her head, soothing her and coaching her breath. Her exhaustive labor began to weaken the birthing process and the baby was not moving down. Dali was nearly incoherent from fatigue and pain.

I began to pray earnestly and saw a vision of a fast-moving train--I told the midwife what I had seen. She said nothing. Suddenly, between Dali's shaking thighs, I saw what appeared to be the crowning head of the baby; but it was not, it was the heel of a tiny foot. The baby was coming as a footling breach, with one foot down and the other leg bent up toward her head.

It was too late to transport Dali the twelve miles to the nearest hospital or to call an ambulance.

The midwife glanced at me and Dali's husband, nodded, then calmly took a gleaming scalpel and sliced into Dali's perineum releasing a gush of blood and a slippery newborn. The baby was immediately passed over to the neonatal attendant, a female farm elder. Our job was now to prevent Dali from bleeding out. At the time, it reminded me of the Dutch boy at the dike. With the midwife's application of multiple compresses, quick stitching and more prayer, the bleeding abruptly stopped. Dali's new daughter was put to her breast; contentedly sucking, the dark-haired infant was oblivious to the near tragedy.

I do not remember driving home that afternoon, bloody, and fully spent. I do remember sobbing uncontrollably as the adrenaline left my brain. By the Grace of God, we had saved the baby and the mother. Thirty years later, Dali has little recollection of the birth.

I do.

Our son had moved into adulthood, leaving his two teen sisters in our double-wide nest. We lived "by faith," which translated into doing whatever needed to be done within the community without pay. I was a volunteer teacher in our private school, teaching my own and other community members' children. We rarely lacked for anything, however, frivolous spending was not in our family's vocabulary.

An affiliate community located in Missouri invited our daughters on an extended summer trip to Chincoteague and elsewhere. They wanted to go but we did not have money for trip clothes, food or souvenirs.

I routinely spent my pre-dawn hours praying and thinking while I jogged a three-mile loop on a dusty, clay road encircling the farm. The crescendos of a frog choir played background music as I passed wild hogs grubbing in damp soil, deer dancing through pines or the occasional alligator croaking from the swamp. This particular morning, I said, "Lord, You know I have no money for the girls' trip. They so want to go. Please come up with something."

Within seconds, I distinctly heard the voiceinmyhead respond: "Go to the McDonald's in Fitzgerald, talk with Jim, the manager, who happens to be a Christian. Offer him $100.00 for all the teenie-beanie babies he has. Promise to pay him any balance you may owe him within one month. Put the teenie-beanie babies on eBay."

Honestly? I rarely went to McDonald's. I did not know what a teenie-beanie baby looked like. Did not know they were then the Happy Meal toy. Did not personally know Jim, the manager. I did have a $100.00 bill stashed in my underwear drawer. By the time I finished my three-mile run, I was eager to fulfill the divine instructions. Without sharing my mission with my family, I inexplicably hopped into my little, blue car and drove to town.

By the time I parked under the golden arches, my heart was racing, and my armpits were damp. At my request, "Jim, your manager" was soon summoned. Flashing my $100 bill, I presented my prescribed proposition: "I don't need the Happy Meals, but I will give you $100.00 for all the teenie-beanie babies you may have. I will pay you any balance owed within one month. "

He briefly pondered my offer. While much of the country was in a crazed frenzy to collect all twelve of the miniature Beanie Babies, NIB (new in bag), local folk were not flocking to our solitary McDonald's for anything other than hamburgers and fries. He had been sent cases of the little plush darlings which stood stacked in his storeroom, taking up valuable supply space. "Okay," he shrugged, reaching for the hundred. We loaded 650 teeny beanie babies, NIB, into my Matrix. I owed Jim $500.00. I had not ever owed anyone that much money.

145

I immediately put them on eBay... at a starting bid of three dollars apiece plus shipping. That night, I received a message from a toy storeowner in Washington, D.C. He was unable to keep the critters on the shelves, there were no more teenie beanie babies to be found in his vicinity, he had been scouring eBay and found me! He offered me five dollars!!!! per teenie beanie baby plus shipping for any number I could send him. The toy store over-nighted the check, I shipped the teenie beanie babies, and paid a shocked Jim full balance within days.

The toy store wanted more.

Clutching my capital, I drove from town to town scoring teenie-beanie babies. The

McDonald's in Vidalia had 650. The day manager insisted that I purchase the entire Happy Meal with each toy. I said, "Okay"

"Really?" he croaked. "Yes," I replied, "I'll tell you what. I will take all the burgers, raw; the French fries frozen in cases; paper bags, drink cups and the teenie-beanie babies. You can keep the soda." It is against the law to sell raw meat, so they began to flip burgers. I waited, and waited, and waited. The shift changed and high-schoolers coming for their afternoon snack stood watching. Three hours later, they were one hundred burgers short. The exhausted young griller beckoned me over to ask humbly, "Ummm, ma'am, would you be willing to take more frozen fries instead of burgers?" Oh, yeah, I would.

The staff paraded boxes of hot, wrapped burgers; three cases of frozen French fries; six hundred-fifty drink cups and six hundred-fifty paper bags stamped with teenie-beanie baby images to my Matrix which soon smelled like a steamy lunch wagon.

I drove home, drooling from the fragrance of my grilled beef-booty. I stacked the frozen French fries in the communal deep-freeze, piled burgers into the school refrigerator for lunches, distributed the remaining burgers among the three communities, sold the teenie beanie paper bags as lots on eBay and used the drink cups until they were gone.

The toy store over-nighted the check, I shipped the teenie beanie babies, and went hunting for more.

By this time, competitor eBay'ers had gotten the revelation and begun hoarding teenie beanie babies for their own profit. I was able to fully complete one more large shipment to the gratitude and applause of the toy storeowner.

I made $13,000 in nine days selling teenie-beanie babies.

The burgers were speedily devoured.

My daughters and I drove ninety miles to the mall, where I treated them to a mad shopping spree while "I Would Walk 500 Miles" poured from store speakers.

The girls loved the Chincoteague ponies.

The symphony of droning cicadas soaring from spindly branches of slash pines, the waves of heat projected from the hot, sandy roads crisscrossing through New

Covenant--summers in South Georgia; hot enough to heat lunch on the hood of a truck.

An hour before sunlight, we were picking 6-inch green beans from Jack-high vines. Swinging machetes, we sliced black-tasseled Silver Queen cobbs from man-height corn stalks. Holding small paring knives, we snipped itchy okra from their tight stems. The rest of the day should have been spent floating in tractor tire tubes under the Spanish moss shade of Gar Lake. But that rarely happened.

I and my team of kitchen kids were cooking for the 2007 July Bowen's Mill Youth Camp. This day, we were relentlessly preparing for the annual Youth Camp Banquet, a coat-n-tie affair which culminated the week's camp activities. We served the camp's daily meals buffet style, laid out on long tables and portioned on individual Styrofoam plates. Youth Camp Banquet was a five-course gourmet meal (i.e. prime rib, chicken cordon bleu, pork tenderloin) served on white china to fancy-dressed teen-agers seated at white linen clothed covered tables. For the campers, it was a really big deal. For us in the kitchen, it was a long, hot day from prep through clean-up.

My mother had been living in her own home at New Covenant for seven years, ever lamenting leaving the poolside of her Florida home. Convention times were the hardest for her, because the kitchen required my full attention, leaving her to the care of neighbors or to fend for herself and her little dog. She hated it and left nothing unsaid.

At ten o'clock that morning, a call came through my vinyl-cased box-phone. I answered to hear my mother's garbled speech interspersed with sobs. I immediately knew she was having a stroke. I delegated imminent tasks, dropped my apron and sped the 2 ½ miles to her home. I found her sitting in her yellow, button-padded swivel chair slumped on the round glass top, which protected a cloth of exploding sunflowers. Her freckled, right arm banged uselessly on her knee, spittle spotting her baby-blue shorts.

Her eyes, once a deadly dark-brown raced frantically behind their cloudy veil, searching to find a way out.

My son and his F-150 were closer than an ambulance. We carried her out and slid her across the wide back seat. He left with horn blaring and lights flashing, while I returned to the kitchen to delegate jobs and locate a kitchen over-seer for the banquet.

It was two hours before I passed through the automatic doors to see my son loudly addressing the ER desk-nurse. He was demanding long-awaited medical attention for his grandmother. I fled to my mother's room to be stabbed by her eyes as she snarled: "It's your fault." I reeled backward, sobbing, into the arms of the ER doctor. He cut-off any chance of my repeating her words with: "It's not your fault. Don't go there."

After two weeks of hospitalization and rehab, although she could speak, my mother had not regained movement in her right side. She stubbornly refused to co-operate with therapy, adamantly claiming that her doctor and nurses were conspiring to euthanize her. I brought her home and, with hospice support, created a hospital environment in her carpeted living room. I found the ordeal of 24-hour caregiving overwhelming and I hired a hospice-recommended health-care worker.

Unbeknownst to both my mother and my new helper, I installed a baby monitor under the hospital bed.

At eight the next morning, I introduced Mary to my mother, led her through the triple-wide maze of rooms, kissed my frowning mother good-bye and went home to listen.

Mary began a cheerful chatter: "Good morning, Mrs. Lewis. Well, I'll be, you are looking lovely this morning. Ah, you don't mind if I remove my wig before I fix your breakfast, do you? How about some coffee and toast?" I could hear Mary humming over the clatter of plates, the sliding of drawers and the perking electric coffee pot. "Now that's a good girl, you ate all your toast. I'm going out on the porch for a smoke, be right back." I was assured that despite my mother's unresponsive, resentful behavior, Mary would continue her daily ministries with the same stream of lighthearted, chatter and loving care.

Mary was an indomitable woman. Her strong, loving arms were the color of rich mahogany. She had never married, had no children and had chosen to devote her life to the care of the dying. Mary had no hair, I never intruded with questions, she never offered. She took her wig off as quickly as she could but kept it within grabbing reach should anyone come to visit my mom. She smoked and smelled like a diesel engine, but she never did it inside the house. Nothing fazed her, nothing surprised her, no one intimidated her. Mary was a rock.

Four weeks into the ordeal, my three children arrived to celebrate their Mima's flamboyant life. Mima feigned gross misery but was visibly delighted by their affectionate attentions. She sucked offered yogurt from a soup spoon and sipped her vodka and tonic through a bendy-straw. It was her happiest day. The children left that evening.

When Mary arrived the next morning, my mother clenched her teeth, refusing to admit food or drink. Our hospice nurse gently removed her dentures and we began to wait. When she became visibly agitated, the hospice nurse applied two morphine patches to the middle of her back, out of reach of her scratching red nails.

My mother slipped into a quiet coma.

It was now the first week of September 2007, six weeks since her stroke. That Friday afternoon, as Mary started out the door for home, she turned and calmly stated, "I am not coming back. Your mama's not gonna last through the weekend. I know these things."

On Saturday morning, my younger brother arrived from Boca Raton. We sat side-by-side on brocade dining chairs; I picked at years of Thanksgiving gravy spills. We watched my mother creaking laboriously through her each shallow breath.

On Sunday morning, my brother left. Ten o'clock service had emptied the general farm populace into church. I was alone with my mother. I padded past her bed to cold white, tile for toast and coffee. My mother exploded into a shrill, enveloping wail that gripped my entire being. She began the same wail, louder. I broke through, rushed to her side and scooped her frailty into my arms.

"I love you, Mom. It's okay, I am here. You can go now, if you wish." Her shuttered eyes flashed two intense, beacons of high-energy light which entered me through my own eyes.

My mother gasped, and she was gone from her body.

I called my husband and hospice. I sat in her kitchen on her yellow, button-padded swivel chair counting sunflowers, safely out of view, and watched as my mother was wheeled to the ambulance waiting in the shade of a wide pecan tree.

In my mother's honor, I am sharing her own family's csirkepaprika recipe:

Ilona's Chicken Paprikash
With love from Mima (Ilona Lewis nie Gyorke)

One whole, plump fryer cut into 8 or 10 pieces
(do not remove skin from the chicken)
1 green pepper sliced thinly
1 yellow onion (not sweet), cut in half and sliced
thinly
1 Roma tomato
Paprika (good brand is imperative, I use Szeged)
1 small container of sour cream Salt to taste
Olive oil enough to lightly cover bottom of a covered
skillet

Scald and peel the tomato, set aside.
Gently sauté onions and green pepper in a bit of oil
until they are glassy. Sprinkle with salt and paprika.
Remove to a bowl.
Lightly brown chicken pieces; sprinkle all pieces, all
sides with about a tablespoon of paprika while
cooking. They should be a nice glowy red.
Put the vegetables back into the pan with the whole,
peeled tomato in the middle.
Cover and cook on low-medium heat, check and turn
the chicken during cooking.
The chicken is done when the drumstick begins to fall
off the bone.

Ladle ¼ cup of the hot juice into a bowl. * Whisk in enough sour cream to make it pink Push the chicken to one side in the pan and blend in the sour cream mix. Serve with traditional noodles, rice or mashed potatoes.

*Note: If the juice appears too watery, remove the chicken and set aside. Gently cook down the juices, restore the chicken and proceed with the sour cream.

Let me know how you like it.

Wherever the ministry traveled within the communities' circuit, they were treated as "kings and priests." The meals were special, the children well behaved, the homes spotless, the tabernacle scrubbed, and everyone came dressed in best for meetings. Traveling ministry rarely experienced the real deal of daily community living.

In the late 1980's, the newly discovered community in Northern Ireland was the rave. Father ministry gave glowing reports of their luxurious accommodations, the spiritual depth of the eldership, the cohesiveness of the residents and man-o-man, the food was fantastic. Why, even the shovels were washed and hung orderly on the barn wall. Buddy had already invited the leading elder, Grae Harris, to stay with us at the big house before accompanying him on a ministry tour.

I had learned to be skeptical of highly praised preachers.

We whirled for days in the attempt to make our guest accommodation and meal menu worthy of Grae's standards. I prepared the guest cabin, dusting, adjusting the sheets just-so, scrubbing the toilet and even left chocolates on the bed. Grae settled in before preaching a fire and brimstone message to the New Covenant family while proclaiming the spiritual superiority of his own community. Most of the men at

155

New Covenant performed hard manual labor and were swift to fall asleep after dinner, as one did, snoring quietly in his chair. Grae stopped his tirade, puffed out his ample chest and gruffly demanded that the man wake up and pay attention or risk losing the blessing of God. We held our Bibles in front of our faces and chortled in amazement.

The next morning, Buddy took Grae on a tour of Bowen's Mill. While they were out, I entered the guest cabin to perform duteous maid service and was met by a suffocating fog of men's cologne. Cigarette stains on the white, porcelain sink revealed that the great spiritual leader had been smoking inside the guest cabin. Smoking is verboten in the Move.

We at the Big House kept many secrets.

Frequently, visiting community "leaders" would approach my husband and me with an invitation to visit their community hoping to lure Buddy's-son from our comfortable lair. Grae attempted the coup with a generous offer to pay our travel expenses to Northern Ireland. We were eager to see his perfect community and graciously accepted his invitation.

It was late winter when we arrived at the Dublin Airport and were chauffeured on the wrong side of the road to Glassdrum Lodge, a cluster of 19th century stone cottages in the idyllic seaside town of Annashort, County Up. The buildings had been converted into a gourmet restaurant and lodge, dormitories and a great dining hall. We were elegantly housed in an upper room with a cozy down covered bed, fluffy pillows and thick towels. I was uncomfortably pregnant, swollen and suffering from jet lag and needed to breathe the crisp, cool Irish air beyond the room's shuttered windows. I managed to open a window and fling back one wooden shutter, which fell from its hinges to clatter uselessly on the pitched roof. My husband advised, "Just leave it there."

After a nap and a warm shower, we anticipated dinner in the dining hall with the farm folk. Not to be. We were not permitted to join the family for any of our meals. While we dined exclusively at the lodge with Grae, his family and a chosen few, the general population ate scraps from the restaurant accompanied by potatoes, lots of potatoes. Our food, rich, saucy and meaty, rough on my pregnant gut, was prepared in the restaurant kitchen. One evening as I discreetly slipped my thick, greasy, gravy smothered pork chop to my husband's plate, Lord Grae gave me a grim, disapproving glare. I wished for a dog under the table.

Before we retired for the night, a young woman politely asked for our breakfast preferences for it was her duty to prepare and deliver our breakfast to our room at our requested time. I politely declined her offer, telling her that we wished to rise early enough to eat with the community. My wish was politely denied. We were instructed to place our shoes in the hallway to be cleaned, polished and returned by morning. Our shoes remained in our room to be worn dirty the next day.

The rationale for Move ministry's infatuation with Grae's community was becoming most apparent.

Glassdrum Lodge operated a bakery, which supplied bread and pastries to their restaurant or sold to local food venues. The bakery, housed in an empty, unheated warehouse, came to life before dawn with the arrival of the farm crew. I was intrigued by the flakey croissants, cheesy Danish and the incredible meat pies and asked the crew if I could accompany them to help and learn the baking process. We wore our coats, bonnets and mittens until the bakery ovens heated the cold, open space. Throughout the long workday, I was awed by the crew's ability to sing, chat and laugh as they created so bountifully in such a miserable setting. From my own recipe file, I had slipped a recipe for potato donuts into my pocket and was honored by their acceptance of my offering which they permanently added to their delectable repertoire.

I figured as much as they ate potatoes, they might as well put them in a yummy, glazed donut.

During most of our days at Glassdrum Lodge, we were left to our own devices, free to roam the small town, shop and sight-see. Although, I was denied further access to the bakery crew, I was determined to get closer to the farm folk and asked Grae if I could be put on the farm schedule. He was suspiciously reluctant and questioned my motive. I told him I was simply bored, antsy, needed something to do and would do anything; why, I'd even scrub his floors. Request granted, and I was soon on my hands and knees, bulging belly hanging low, cheerfully singing and scrubbing the bricked Lodge entryway with a small hand brush. Chatter of my position rattled through the camp.

I'd become an unexpected heroine.

The time of our departure arrived not a minute too soon for me. The car was loaded and, as we said our fond farewells to everyone, Grae's absence was noted. Without revealing that his commitment to pay our travel expenses had not yet been fulfilled, I insisted we wait to tell Grae good-bye. As valuable minutes ticked away, he finally appeared, check in hand, mumbled his proper adieu and turned away.

Grae Harris never returned to Bowen's Mill and he never bothered with us again. It was after our visit that his reign toppled, and his people left to establish a new community in Southern Ireland.

My husband became more distant as my life embraced three children, farm chores, schedules and teaching school. He was attempting to establish himself as an effective elder in the Move with a hope of becoming part of the traveling ministry. I was happy and content to do what I was doing; I was with my children; my days were full, and I slept very well.

Then a man entered our lives. John was a younger man whose Austrian father and Quaker mother were frequent convention boarders in our home. My son had grown and gone, making his room available for extended guests. John came and stayed, showering me and my girls with rare male attention. I found it extremely flattering.

John invited Ryan and me on an extended European tour to visit his relatives in Austria and my cousin in Germany before traveling to Move communities in Wales and southern Ireland. My husband graciously accepted the all-expenses-paid offer, and we soon found ourselves, without children, flying Virgin Atlantic to London. While sitting between the two men on the plane, I was mildly amused when John slid his hand under my thigh to stroke my leg. The amusement turned to confusion as intimacy and an emotional draw intensified throughout the three-week journey. Thankfully, I never succumbed to a physical affair with John. The trip ended, and John went home, leaving my mind in turmoil.

John entered a Move community in southwest Florida and arranged to meet me and my daughters during our visit to my mother's home in Deerfield Beach. It was there that John chose to reveal himself — literally. He joined us in my mother's kidney shaped pool and hung by his arms from the deep end edge. While my girls and I played Marco Polo I became disturbingly aware that John was dangling from the pool's edge wearing no swim trunks. Without any explanation, I hurried the girls out of the pool and I fled into the house after them. John left claiming an unexpected appointment. I persuaded myself that I did not see what I thought I saw and did not tell anyone of the incident. We continued our friendship with John's family.

Less than a year later, during a visit to John's parents, he molested my daughter, Angela, then 14, by creeping into her bed, fondling her and rubbing his penis against her. He convinced her that it was their special little secret. She kept their secret until I caught him in another attempt two years later. My heart was sick. When confronted, John vehemently denied the first incident and he asked forgiveness for the second. My husband did not press him and accepted his apology without further questioning. I said and did nothing. I do not know why I did not file a police report.

Angela sought counsel from her grandfather, whose response was that she must have done something to "ask for" the molestations. This was the pact ministerial response to any allegation of sexual abuse. The next response was a question: "Do you believe God has you where He wants you? If so, then what has happened is the perfect will of God for you."

My husband and I decided that a change of environment would benefit our family and our marriage. It seemed that the Lord was drawing us to the community in Blessington, Ireland.

Postscript: At age 29, Angela wrote a letter to John's new wife telling her of the molestations and expressing concern for the woman's young daughter, John's stepdaughter. The woman's reply was one of honest gratitude; however, John denied the acts blaming the accusations on Angela's adolescent imagination.

Glasdrum residents operated the five-star hotel, gourmet restaurant, bakery and taxi service which supported their large population of families and single adults. They allowed Grae to house children separately in boys' and girls' dormitories and to grant elders special privileges. When multiple allegations of abuse were voiced, Grae's personal accountant, Drew, secretly arranged and conducted a mass exodus of the people to Humperdink House in Southern Ireland. The primarily English congregation accepted their liberator, Drew, as their chosen elder-in-charge.

Humperdink House, the center of the community, is a four-story stone mansion built in 1750. The basement contains the kitchen, dining hall and laundry room. The first floor is dominated by the farm office, a banquet room with 12-foot draped windows, a plant-filled conservatory, and a schoolroom. The top two floors are housing for families and singles. Residents, guests, and workers shared few bathing rooms. (Never a problem because the farm rule was one bath/shower per week per person.) There were several outbuildings used as residences, barns to house milk cows, sheep and chickens, a root cellar and a centrally placed garden plot.

Ryan and I had been charmed by our previous visit to Humperdink House and presented our leading to move there to Buddy and the New Covenant elders. With little discussion and their unanimous blessing, we packed our bedding and belongings into eight olive-green military duffle bags and, with our two daughters, flew the friendly skies to Dublin.

Prior to being assigned permanent housing, we were ensconced in spacious guest quarters on the second floor of the main house with a private bathroom and a deep-footed tub. Our daughters had a smaller, separate room which shared a communal shower "down the hall."

That first night, suffering from jet lag and over-stuffed by the communal dinner of fried potatoes and baked chicken, we fell into deep slumber. We were expected to rise early for the morning praise service at 6:30 A.M.

I awoke at four, rejuvenated and ready to explore our new surroundings. I determined that I had plenty of time to take a run, shower, wake the girls and make the 6:30 event. Ryan, concerned for my safety, accompanied me and, on our return, he prepared to shower in the shared shower while I used our private tub. Soap, shampoo, and towel in hand, Ryan flicked an outlet switch to turn on a filled electric coffee pot before he left our room. Listening for the welcome gurgle of fresh coffee, I slid into the warm footed tub and immediately smelled smoke as a grey cloud crept under the closed bathroom door. I leaped from the tub and flung open the door to view flames bursting from a towel left hanging over an electric space heater in our bedroom. Ryan's large fingers had inadvertently hit the heater's outlet switch rather than the coffee pot. The flaming towel threatened long, gloomy, brocade drapes hanging too near an antique, wooden armoire. Vividly realizing that I was stark, raving naked I did not want anyone running to my cry of "FIRE!" Instead of bellowing, I yanked the electrical cord from the wall, scooped the flaming towel into my wet arms, plunged it into the tub water and then threw the sopping towel over the smoldering space heater.

We were early for the 6:30 praise service. Dottie sent a luxurious set of plush burgundy towels to replace the one we had destroyed.

We moved from our temporary guest quarters in the main house into two bedrooms of a two-story, farm constructed A-frame house adjacent to the garden area. We were without furniture and slept on floor-bound air mattresses, which we had transported in our duffel bags. There was no heat in our rooms; the house was not insulated; and sound flowed freely through every room, upstairs and downstairs. Next to our bedroom window was an open gap, which permitted a constant draft of Irish winter dampness forcing Ryan and me to sleep in our hooded parkas. The girls' room, though without a draft, was still very cold. I asked for an electric space heater to keep our girls warm at night.

I learned that no one else on the farm had a heater in their bedroom. I was tacitly informed that "being cold" was an admittance of carnal weakness to be overcome with spiritual strength and not a heater. Our girls were deemed the carnal, spoiled Americans, Buddy Cobb's granddaughters. We were given a space heater and we reimbursed Humperdink House for the "extra electricity."

It was not long before I was called into my first elders' meeting to sit demurely within their circle of chairs as the unstated policy of "a bath a week" was explained to me. Someone had heard me taking GI showers after my morning runs. (GI shower: turn on water, get wet, shut off water, soap up, turn on water, rinse quickly). I had also insisted that my daughters maintain their Southern hygiene by taking a sink bath after their daily work of cooking, cleaning and barn chores. Drew openly charged me with using too much hot water. I reminded him that the farm water came from their own deep well and ran through a pipe heated by the large, stoked wood furnace. He sighed deeply, and we continued our daily bathing routines.

The lack of adequate laundry facilities in the main house prompted the women to layer wet laundry across radiators lining the stone-walled halls. The resulting humidity rose to speckle the ceilings with dark mold. My older daughter developed a thick, bronchial cough from over-exposure to the cold, damp weather and the moldy house. Every evening, my husband laid her on the wood floor and pounded her back to relieve the heavy congestion in her chest. Our beloved pediatrician, Dr. Dora, mailed us antibiotics from Georgia and cautioned us to prioritize her health. Our daughter continued to make the back-and-forth trek from our house to the main house to attend school, meet her work schedule and eat communal meals, however, once she came home in the evening, I kept her inside and put her to bed.

I was called into my second elders' meeting. We sat in the same circle and Drew questioned my non-attendance at after-dinner get-togethers held in a sitting room of the main house. I had not been informed of any mandatory meetings and was completely taken off-guard. I explained my reluctance to take my sick daughter out into the dank evenings. Drew solemnly asserted that she would be healed more quickly if she spent more time with the "spiritual family." I disagreed and was riled by his next suggestion that I leave her home alone while I attended the meetings. I can still taste the words that flew from my mouth: "Why, Brother Drew? Are you going to take my attendance star from me?"

We continued to stay home in the evenings. My lack of compliance began to gather its consequences.

Even though we resided in the A-frame, I was assigned to clean all eight latrines in the main house. Rather than bitch and moan, I sang heartily as I wandered from toilet to toilet. "I am the lovely loo lady, lovingly coming to Lysol your loo! Excuse me, please, as I lovingly Lysol your loo!" Soon I was being addressed as the "lovely loo lady."

The daily scrubbing of the tiled foyer became another assigned chore, to be completed cheerfully while lugging a stringy rag mop and bucket of

Pinesol water. The entrance hall of the main house was laid in shiny, white tile floor, which rarely dried in the damp air before someone tracked footprints across it. I prompted a distinguished visitor into gales of laughter when I ordered him to take off his shoes and walk in his dress socks over my newly, mopped floor. Drew removed me from the foyer mopping detail.

I and my daughter were awarded the daily responsibility of preparing the basis of the Humperdink diet, fifty pounds of potatoes. The large, white Irish potatoes were preserved in the depths of a dark root cellar and buried in muck gathered from animal stalls. Farm boys lugged the nearly-frozen potatoes to the kitchen in five-gallon buckets where they were dumped into a deep-sink of warm water. We wore rubber gloves to protect our hands from the filth and cold as we brushed each potato. After the initial scrubbing, the potatoes were rewashed, rinsed and left draining as we peeled and diced into pots of clean, salted water. I loathed the job. My hands ached with cold, my clothing became wet and dirty and the peeler was never sharp enough. I was not happy my daughter had to participate but I refused to share my misery. Instead, I composed The Peeling Potato Song: "Oh, how I love peeling potatoes. Peeling potatoes is what I love! Oh, how I love peeling potatoes." Others heard me singing and to my immense delight, women volunteered to assist us in potato peeling.

On Saturday mornings, individual couples were scheduled to prepare a special breakfast of their choice limited only by a budgeted allotment. When Ryan and I were granted a turn, we were excited and happily padded farm funds with our own monies. I purchased butter, sugar, sausage, cinnamon and eggs with the intent of livening up the basic breakfast fare of stale, dry toast and cold boiled eggs (one per, please). It made breakfast of the year as people sprinkled sugar and cinnamon on heavily buttered toast accompanied by fluffy, scrambled eggs and sausage.

I was called into a third elders' meeting. The elder-lady in charge of the kitchen accused me of stealing additional farm eggs for my lavish amount of scrambled breakfast eggs. I had not kept my grocery receipt and was unable to substantiate my innocence. It was further presumed that I had used the breakfast as an occasion to gain favor from the people and incite them against the eldership.

Nevertheless, I gained the love and trust of the general Humperdink House community. They had escaped a cruel "Christian" dictatorship in the North to fall under the rule of the religious authoritarian who had saved them. They were bound to Drew by what he had done for them. I was an enigma who did not fit their preconception of Buddy Cobb's daughter-in-law, and that continued to amuse them. We only had problems with the elders.

Humperdink's elders did not recognize my husband as a fellow elder because he was from "Carnal" Covenant, his marriage was unstable, and he obviously could not control his wife. My daughters were frustrated by our work schedule, the miserable weather and their inability to befriend their English peers. It was a difficult time for us as a couple and as a family.

God moved in strange and mysterious ways.

The Move had a college in Brussels, Belgium. To supplement their curriculum, the students had the opportunity to travel and board at Move communities in Great Britain, Spain and Switzerland. During their visit to Humperdink House, a shy, nineteen-year-old American tugged at Ryan's arm and asked to speak to him privately. He revealed that an elder's wife had made inappropriate advances to him; the boy was embarrassed and did not know how to discourage her without causing a loud scandal.

Hiding under blankets to stifle our voices, Ryan and I made a clandestine, middle-of-the-night telephone call to Buddy who advised Ryan to speak directly to Drew. The ensuing conversation with Drew did not go well. Ryan was accused of spreading libelous rumors in retaliation for not being accepted as a bona fide elder.

I discovered that someone had apparently entered our private quarters, searched our belongings and rummaged through our personal correspondence. I gathered all our letters, financial papers and mail and burned them in the voluminous wood furnace.

Ryan placed another overseas midnight call to Buddy. Dottie and Lee Fife entered the discussion; their consensus was for us to gracefully leave Humperdink House and return to the States.

"Humperdink House"

Formal Dining in Ireland

Ilona was the lovely Czech widow of a noted Irish poet. After his untimely death, she lived under a veil of guilt for having had a steamy affair before losing her husband. For this, she had sought penance by attending services at Humperdink House where she met Drew. Attracted by her expressive, doe-like eyes, Drew picked up the mantle of widow's helper and housed Ilona and her two children in a single-wide "caravan" parked on the back driveway of Humperdink House.

Ilona and I developed a friendship based on our cultural similarities, our children's compatibility and our shared repugnance to the English ways forced upon us at Humperdink House. After quickly completing our assigned farm chores, we would often take our four children on excursions to surrounding towns for candy and ice cream treats.

One unusually sunny Irish day, while the children were in school, she and I hurried through our work schedule and slipped away to a near pub for a cheese sandwich and a beer. We giggled as the completely male clientele ceased from their chattering gossip to turn from their mugs and stare as we, in our long denim skirts, sashayed to the bar, perched primly on barstools and ordered a pint.

Although, I was not called into an elders' meeting, Drew pulled me aside to tell me that I was not a good influence on Ilona. He forbade us to complete our scheduled tasks ahead of time. If we were scheduled for two hours of cleaning toilets, we were to take the entire two hours to clean toilets.

In the attempt to discourage our developing relationship, the eldership began to quietly shun Ilona and her children. The farm kitchen ceased making concessions for her daughter's multiple food allergies making mealtimes exasperating and dangerous for the young girl. This unkind development caused Ryan to assume a stronger role as Ilona's white knight and they became uncomfortably close.

After Buddy advised us to leave Humperdink House, Ilona decided she and her children would return to the Czech Republic. We opted to travel with her to Prague and stay with her relatives while touring the city; after which, we followed her to her flat in Dundalk, an Irish border town. While our children enjoyed their playmates' company, I watched in dismay as my husband became more intimate with my good friend.

One night, I had a vivid dream that Ilona crawled into our bed to lay between me and Ryan. I discussed the dream with my husband and we knew it was time to return to the States. We flew back to Georgia and reclaimed our doublewide at New Covenant.

Two years later, against the counsel of the New Covenant elders, but with my blessing, Ryan returned to Ireland to spend ten days with Ilona. He professed that she was his soulmate and he had wanted to stay with her. He did not stay but he should have had.

After our return from Ireland, we resettled into our double-wide mobile home at New Covenant and life resumed as before.

When the job of Administrator of Bowen's Mill Convention Center became open, I was already managing the convention kitchen and encouraged Ryan to volunteer to fill the vacated position. Since his dad was president of the Bowen's Mill Christian Center Board of Directors, it was easy to gain the approval of the entire father ministry. Ryan became the Administrator of Bowen's Mill Convention Center and I became Secretary of the Board.

Meanwhile, Stu Allen, his wife, four children and their nanny entered the Move in New York, and too quickly attempted the big leap into community at Bowen's Mill. Through their shared fascination with the stock market, Ryan and Stu became fast friends. However, within a short time, Stu acknowledged that he and his family were not cutout for communal living and off they went to Montana, had a fifth child, separated and divorced.

Stu married their nanny, had a baby girl, and, taking the last child of his first wife, relocated to Florida. Stu had maintained communication with my husband and when things failed financially, it was Ryan who convinced him to return to Bowen's Mill with his new family. They moved into a house next door to ours at New Covenant. Despite my voiced indignation over his divorce, his new wife, Ann, and I forged our own friendship.

One fateful morning, while digging a ditch under the hot sun, Stu suffered a fatal heart attack. Buddy said it was God's judgment.

Immediately upon Stu's death, Ryan took on the Biblical responsibility of caring for his widow, Ann, and their two children. As Convention Center administrator, he subcontracted Ann to perform the less physically taxing tasks of pre and postconvention maintenance of on-site accommodations. The board approved a worthy wage and, in addition, being part of the full-time convention staff, Ann's personal utility bills, car fuel and other household expenses were covered by convention offerings and donations.

Ryan's deepening involvement with Ann and her family became apparent enough to raise eyebrows within the community, prompting several to confidentially warn me and him of rising suspicions. Ryan brushed off all concerns and increased his interaction with Ann.

My husband was not alone in his attraction to Ann's gentle manner, hospitable habits and radiant smile. She gained a serious suitor in the newly widowed owner of the sawmill, Wells Paul.

Through our kitchen window, we watched Wells arrive at six every morning for a walk and coffee with Ann. This daily ritual irritated my husband to the point that he began to wait on the porch, pacing in and out of the house until Wells finally drove away.

Ann declined Wells' proposal which ended the morning rendezvous and appeased my husband.

New Covenant gained a new family from a city group. Thelma, an attractive, outgoing Guatemalan woman; her younger Mexican husband, Juan; and their two children were hardly settled when my husband presented himself at their doorstep. Their daughter, Lisa, was a selective mute who spoke only to her immediate family. With the conviction that Lisa was under demonic influence, the elders initially balked at admitting Lisa to the Bowen's Mill school unless her parents consented to the Move method of "spanking her into submission." Selective mutes do not respond well to strict disciplinary actions, and the girl absolutely refused to speak. I prayed for unthreatening, gentler means of coercing her into oral communication and offered to integrate Lisa into my combined class of fifth and sixth grades.

I seated Lisa next to Frances, an exceptionally bright and intuitive curly locked ten-year-old. I allowed Lisa to raise her hand and answer yes or no questions with a nod or a headshake. On her own volition, Lisa began whispering her responses into Frances' ear and I nonchalantly accepted Frances as Lisa's mouthpiece. Eventually, the whispers became hushed verbal communication, easily heard by the entire class. Within weeks, Lisa was speaking normally within the walls of our classroom. If anyone entered our room or if Lisa stepped over our threshold, she would become silent.

As a convention preparation loomed before me, I asked Thelma if Lisa could assist in the convention kitchen after school. Lisa happily became my kitchen shadow, chattering freely as we worked; becoming mute if anyone other than her classmates or family appeared in the kitchen doorway. Her parents were thrilled at the steady progression of open communication and wholly supported my teaching procedures and relationship with their daughter.

Honestly, I was the most amazed by the results of my endeavors.

Through my personal efforts with Lisa, Thelma and I became friends. My husband and I began to socialize with them in our homes with shared dinners and evening whiskey-laced lattes. I was impressed with Thelma's intelligence, multi-lingual abilities and computer literacy and subsequently made an appeal to the board of directors that she join the convention staff as the reservationist, a position which required linguistic and computer skills. Our shared social times expanded to the convention center.

Meanwhile, Ann was discreetly courted by a gentleman who had been contracted to renew the concrete floor of the convention kitchen. Ryan openly sulked through the courtship until their marriage was imminent.

With Ann's impending departure from the convention staff, Thelma began finagling her way into the maintenance work, quietly re-doing what Ann had already finished. I watched contention grow between the two women as they subtly vied for my husband's attentions. After Ann's marriage and departure, Ryan and Thelma began spending more "convention related time" together. Coffee moments became long Biblical discussions, which I found tiresome and uninspiring; I ceased participating. The frequency of lengthy **tête-à-têtes** became disconcerting enough for me to approach her husband. Juan claimed he "was fine" with their friendship.

Until he cracked.

One evening, we received a distressing call from Thelma. After a heated argument, Juan had fled into the New Covenant woods surrounding a deep pond. Ryan and I were familiar with the woods and we walked in different directions searching for Juan. I found him leaning against a slender slash pine just a few yards from the pond. His usually bright, dark eyes stared vacantly, his head hung limply to one side, his tongue drooped from his mouth while spittle ran from his lip staining his white t-shirt. My first thought was that he was having a stroke; I yelled for help but received no response.

I approached Juan and gently stroked his hair, asking him if he was okay; he muttered, "Yes." I held his arm to ease him off the tree, wiped the drool from his chin with his shirt and encouraged him to walk with me. I did not call out for fear of startling him. We moved slowly as I questioned what had provoked him to run into the woods. He confided that he and Thelma had argued about her increasing times alone with Ryan. I asked him no more as I led him safely home. Ryan insisted that I not relate the troubling event to Buddy or the elders. I did not. Juan later dismissed the incident as never happening.

Once again, farm members cautioned Ryan and me about his friendship with Thelma. Once again, he brushed off concerns and continued. When I expressed my own discomfort to Ryan's parents, Buddy summoned the four of us to a private meeting in which he bluntly asked if there had been a sexual encounter to which Ryan and Thelma snickered and answered, "No!"

That was it, it was settled, no sexual encounter, no reason to fret. Meeting adjourned. Their friendship continued and deepened, causing further disquiet in the community until someone finally complained to the father ministry.

At the next convention, Ryan and I were invited to a meeting with elders from the three Bowen's Mill communities, father ministry and their wives. We sat on opposite sides of the large circle as they interrogated us concerning observations from across our communities. I was accused of being over-reactive and responded by rising from my seat, calling the proceedings "bull shit" and walked out.

As Ryan and Thelma's affinity continued, there were other meetings, there was marriage counseling and there were loving attempts from Move members to reconcile us. All of which failed.

In October 2009, Ryan and I sat in the living room of our doublewide. He asked me, "What do you want me to do?" I answered, "I want you to lay down your relationship with Thelma." He responded, "God is not requiring me to do that." To which I answered, "Well, then, God is requiring me to leave."

After living in community for 32 years and married for 39 years, I left. I was fifty-seven years old.

I was not always a Cobb.

I first met Dottie and Buddy on a snowy February day in Berlin, Germany. They and their youngest child had flown from Miami to attend our wedding. They had learned of our relationship through a brief recorded communication from their draftee son. Having assumed that I was a little German hippie girl looking for an American husband, they were somewhat relieved to discover that I was a little American hippie military brat infatuated with their only son, Ryan.

Following Ryan's military discharge six months later, we moved into their spacious Hollywood Hills, Florida, ranch style home. During eight months of intimately sharing her home with us, Dottie treated me as a daughter. Despite her looks of disapproval, she allowed me to teach swimming in their pool attired only in a bikini. Upon her learning of my culinary skills, she encouraged me to create unleashed in her immaculate kitchen. Unleashed it was, for as a teen-aged cook, I was not in the habit of "keeping things clean and tidy."

Other than cooking, I possessed minimal domestic skills. My mother had been my wardrobe designer and seamstress. She had created my lacey, wedding dress on her vintage, foot pump Singer. However, she did not teach me how to sew. When I was given the high school elective of Home Economics, my mother marched into the principal's office and let him know she did not send me to school to learn how to cook and clean; then yanked me out of the class. It was Dottie who patiently taught me how to sew, crochet, quilt and clean house.

We moved from Buddy's house to an apartment complex near downtown Hollywood before purchasing our Afghan Hound, Hussan. He was our firstborn and Dottie acknowledged him as such, tolerating his antics of spreading toilet trash, including used tampons, down her hallway; nearly chewing his way through a closed, wooden pocket door and gnawing the cover off her favorite devotional book. Hussan was never banned from her home.

Our son was born in 1973, eight months after Dottie's first grandchild, Lynn. She became a full-fledged grandmother who never refused a baby-sitting request and often happily kept both babies while we partied.

A fond memory is the evening we left the toddler cousins with Dottie while we four parents traipsed to Steak and Ale for unlimited pitchers of beer and sangria with our steaks. We ate and drank and drank and drank, never giving a thought to the time because of a wide window view streaming sunlight into the restaurant. Eventually, patrons began to thin out, the staff began clearing tables and setting chairs upside down on the table-tops. After questioning the time and apparent sunlight, we learned it was merely a convincing semblance of a sunny window view. It was after eleven when we sheepishly picked-up the fed, bathed and slumbering babies. Dottie only shook her head and accepted our drunken apologies.

Buddy and Dottie's grandparent status boasted eight grandchildren, four girls and four boys. They often invited all eight of the kids, sans parents, to join them at their summer time-share in Cashiers, North Carolina. The children loved the time with their grandparents, as did we! I recently asked my forty-five-year-old son what it was they so enjoyed about spending that time with their grandparents. He replied, "Mom, they would feed us breakfast, then drop us off at the Country Club until Grandpa came back to get us for supper. We had a blast!"

My two daughters were born in the house we shared with Buddy and Dottie. Home births demand concentration and cool headedness no matter what may happen. Dottie attended both girls' births; her job at my side was as neonatal caregiver. She received the newborn, cleaned her, monitored her body functions and cuddled her until the baby was put to my breast. She was my strong confidence that my infant was in the best care.

I taught in our small private school for many years. If one of my own children were ill, I would leave them home with Dottie while I taught. She would kneel by their side and pray for quick recovery and minister to their woes with homemade vanilla custard and cold, mommy-forbidden Coca Colas.

Sometimes, I thought the kids feigned sickness just to spend that indulgent time with Grandma.

Despite her occasional "spoiling" the children, Dottie completely supported my discipline. If she thought I was wrongly handling the children, she would confront me privately. She never allowed the children to witness disagreement between her and me concerning them.

Due to health issues, my mother moved into our community in 2000. Although, my mom refused to become a member of the church, Dottie often neglected her own schedule to accommodate befriending her. Weather permitting, the two grandmas would meet at the community swimming pool for laps and conversation. Dottie often popped into my mother's home for brief chit chats. I did not have to ask Dottie to do this, she just did it.

When I chose to leave her son, she did not abandon me. She continued to love me and consider me as her daughter. When she became ill, she wanted me to attend her. When I was able to go to her side, she accepted me as was.

My father passed at age 58 from diabetes related complications. My son was two years old when Buddy became his only grandfather. They shared an intimate loving relationship until Buddy's death, as did I, as his favorite daughter-in-law, his only daughter-in-law.

Buddy never wavered in his conviction that God had directed him to support us financially. I often resented his generosity as coddling his son. He would answer my complaints with a gentle smile and a shrug and continued to pour his personal blessings into our coffer.

I would jokingly remind him that although he was not always right, he was never wrong.

I have heard the rumors of Buddy's "lavish" lifestyle funded by church donations. Buddy poured personal earnings from his airline days and personal investments into numerous Move communities, Bowen's Mill and overseas missions. If anyone had a need, Buddy was the first to empty his pockets. He did receive church donations while traveling and preaching, which helped cover his travel expenses and enabled him to give his time and energy to the church.

Buddy had a one-track mind which centered on his own Biblical convictions. Buddy believed what he believed, and that was that.

When our marriage began to falter, he urged me to hang-in-there, and he never relinquished his faith in his son's integrity. I suspected that deep inside, he did not want to admit what was obvious. It would have violated his convictions.

Many from the Move have commented to me, "YOU did not have to live the way WE did on the farms. You are a Cobb."

Well, they are right in so many ways. We lived in a fishbowl, our family was never to slip, falter or fail, and, when we did, it was the evening news.

"Your children never seemed to lack. You always seemed to have money."

Buddy gave us a minimal monthly stipend. We had no mortgage. My husband and I received random monetary gifts from others. I had several outside paying jobs (as did my husband), including house cleaning, light construction, face painting, accounting and work at the sawmill. If we had medical needs or personal necessities, I prayed. And that worked; it still works.

"You had travel advantages that others did not have."

Yes, we did. We were frequently courted by other Move ministries to relocate to their community. They paid our travel expenses and boarded us in fine style. It was their attempt to coup a Cobb.

"Your family did not suffer mental, physical or sexual abuse."

My own children were exposed to abuse of every kind. Did I feel it was God's perfect plan for them? No. Did I report to the authorities? No. Why? I really have no answer. I would now do otherwise.

"Do you believe the stories of sexual molestation and harsh disciplinary methods used on the farms during the early days of the Move?"

Yes, I do. Unfortunately, few are the alleged victims that have come forward. The statute of limitations has swallowed opportunity for many cases. My heartfelt desire is for Move ministry to openly acknowledge past abuse and ask forgiveness from those violated. I sincerely hope that any form of abuse has been eradicated from existing Move communities and groups.

Buddy and Dottie

Glossary of Sorts

Although not in alphabetical order, this section defines terms, idioms, phrases, examples of the "Man-child Speech." It also clarifies some doctrines and beliefs of the Move.

Five-fold ministry: According to scripture (Eph. 4:11) and as exemplified by our five-fingered hand, there are five ministerial positions in the church: apostles, prophets, teachers, evangelists and pastors (or shepherds). The Move gives rank to apostles, or father ministry, as being of the highest spiritual caliber. Teachers are teachers of any sort, whether kitchen, airfield or classroom. The Move considers evangelists as unnecessary because the Bible states: "By this shall all men know that ye are my disciples, if ye have love one to another." (John 13:35). No more need for an evangelist so long as we are loving each other. Pastors are the shepherds of the flock, they bring God's Word to the people and govern. Prophets have a gift to receive the Word of God through channeling, visions and dreams.

Seeking words: There are no personal decisions in the Move. Important life decisions regarding a job, having children, buying a car or home, deciding a course of medical treatment, etc. are taken to the elders, as a "leading," which is a preconception of the desired outcome.

An example: A couple has a leading to build a home. They present their leading to their local elders. The elders consider the leading before asking three prophets to "pray for a couple" without revealing any other information. A prophet's word can be disqualified if he/she has insider information. Each prophet prays to ask God for a word specifically for a couple. The word will come to a prophet through a vision, a dream, or a voice. The prophets transcribe their individual word and all three words are submitted to the elders. The elders read, reread and review each word; they discuss the situation as framed by the spiritual content of each word, before declaring their combined opinion.

The couple is invited to an elders' meeting, where they will sit with the elders as the three words are dramatically read aloud. An elder will then declare their unanimous opinion of God's ruling. The couple is free to accept or decline the elders' counsel. However, if they choose to decline the elders' counsel, they are sternly cautioned against "missing God" and possibly losing God's blessing on their endeavor.

Walking out a year: A man and a woman have "feelings" for one another with the intention of beginning a romantic relationship. Protocol requires them to go to an elder and let him/her know of their budding relationship. The elder takes the news to the eldership of their community or group; after which the couple is asked into an elder's meeting. Because the Move does not sanction dating, close friendships between sexes or going steady, the elders may agree that the couple "walk out a year." During this year, there is no physical contact, no time alone without a chaperone, no talk of love or romance, and absolutely no kissing. If the couple manages to conclude the years' time with complete adherence to the mandates imposed up them, and the elders decide that they are ready for marriage, the elders will then seek words to confirm their leading to wed. After the prophets submit the words to the elders, the elders review the words and come to their unanimous decision of: Yes, the couple can marry; no, they cannot marry; or they must extend the year to further mature their relationship.

Sin: In addition to sins listed in the Bible, sinning can be defined as thinking or doing something that goes against Move teaching. To name a few: Listening to secular music. Homosexuality or bisexuality. Watching television or movies containing violence, homosexuality, sex, vulgarity, nudity, alcohol or drug use. Spending "too much" time watching or participating in sports; especially if it means missing a service or Bible study. Missing any church or Bible study for any reason other than acute illness.

If one sees a brother in sin, one has an obligation to warn the sinner. If the sinner does not heed the warning and cease, the elders become involved. If sin continues, the sinner is ostracized from the church.

Some sin, such as sexual molestation, has been effectively concealed to protect the church. The ministry contends that there are no victims in cases of sexual misconduct. There are only perpetrators (of any age) who send sexual messages to one who is "weak" and responds to his/her weakness with inappropriate behavior. The Move teaches that ALL things are ordered by God, including physical, sexual or mental abuse.

At times, the solution is to send the weaker vessel to another community, where he/she has a second chance to change the behavior. Law enforcement is never involved.

Years ago, when our son was a young adolescent, a male elder and his wife moved into a home next to ours. Lee Fife advised me not to allow my son to be alone with the man. When I asked why, her response was, "Because he likes little boys." I was horrified to understand that she knew this man was a child molester, and, yet, the ministry had approved his relocation to our community.

Carnal man: Poke your arm. That is the carnal man, it is also the flesh man and his desires.

Yielding to the flesh: When one gives in to carnal desire such as gluttony, promiscuity, smoking or other such vices. These addictions, or weaknesses of the flesh, may require deliverance and guided spiritual maintenance.

Living by faith: Believing that God supplies all needs.

Farms: A Move community is commonly referred to as a farm. Each farm is registered as a church. The farm owns the property. The home residents may or may not own their house depending on the community's organization. Each farm is autonomous in its government and finances.

Covering: A spiritual blanket that is meant to protect and instruct. Parents cover their own children. Teachers cover students. A chaperone covers a couple's time together.

Elders: The governing, covering group of men and women who have shown themselves spiritually worthy of the position of an elder. A group of elders, or eldership, governs each farm or city group. Elderships make determinations based on their interpretation of prophetic words, or on their united thoughts. Elders come under the covering of the traveling and father ministries.

Traveling ministry: Male or female elders living in community who are invited to preach at city groups or other communities. Traveling ministry expenses are usually supplemented by church offerings and donations. Traveling ministry come under the covering of the father ministry.

Father Ministry: The core group of men who travel through Move congregations worldwide preaching a consistent thread of Word. Father Ministry descend

195

from the original two founders, Sam and Buddy. Existing father ministry make the determination as to who is to become a new member of the father ministry. All father ministries are on the Board of Directors at Bowen's Mill Christian Center, Inc. Father ministry have the authority to preach, counsel, approve upcoming elders, hear and settle grievances at any Move location. Father ministry do not need an invitation to visit a farm or city group and they preach at most global conventions. Father ministry's travel expenses are supplemented by church offerings and donations.

Bowen's Mill Christian Center: There are four properties associated with Bowen's Mill in Ben Hill County, Georgia:

Bowen's Mill Convention Center is the largest of the properties, encompassing several hundred acres including dense woods, lodging accommodations, campground, three meeting halls, a commercial kitchen, pole-barn dining area and sport fields. http://bowensmill.org/

The Ridge, dedicated to the care of those in need of mental or physical assistance, sits at the site of a former Civilian Conservation Corp (CCC) camp high on a sand ridge on the south side of House Creek, separating it from the Convention Center. Ridge property includes a cemetery containing the gravesites of Move members.

The Bowen's Mill school located on Highway 129, now closed, contains a series of buildings, which was once a restaurant, country store and hotel. https://vanishingsouthgeorgia.com/tag/bowens-mill-ga/

Family Farm adjoins the Convention Center property. Originally intended for the homes of those who worked at the Convention Center, its numbers have fallen to very few residents, of which only two are associated with work at the Convention Center.

New Covenant Fellowship, a fifth property, in Wilcox County, is located two miles north of the Convention Center. Originally purchased by Buddy Cobb and his brother-in-law. Buddy eventually bought his brother-in-law's share and subsequently leased the bigger portion to the church of New Covenant. Buddy maintained ownership of the Big House, surrounding out-buildings and the pecan orchard. Since Buddy's death, the leased portion has been deeded to New Covenant.

Despite internet rumors, there is no and never was a functioning airstrip at Bowen's Mill. Those few ministries who once owned their own planes hangered at the Fitzgerald Municipal Airport.

Northern Farms: Communities in Alaska and Canada, which were etched out of the wilderness during the late 1970's into the '80's. Few are still active and populated.

http://whitestonecommunityassociation.net
https://www.facebook.com/Whitestone-Farms-143058369109259/
https://en.wikipedia.org/wiki/The_Move_(Sam_Fife)
https://youtube/uzX7B-f0XVk
https://babygrapes.wordpress.com/2014/11/26/holidays-the-sanctified-andunholy/#more-109

Covenant Life College: A four-year non-accredited college founded to provide further education for children who had been schooled in the Move. The original campus located in Brussels, Belgium, was closed and relocated to Bowen's Mill, Georgia with a branch at Whitestone Farms in Alaska. The Georgia campus was closed sometime in the 1990's. As of this writing, Whitestone's branch is still operating and is presumably open to the public.
https://covenantlifecollege.net/aboutus.html

IMA: International Ministerial Association: The licensing agent of the Move. All elders are card-carrying members of IMA, which identifies them as pastors. IMA regulates the closed email system used by the Move.

IMA's Doctrinal Statement: www.ima.cc

Thank you for reading
We Walk on Water by Cara Cobb
Please post a review on Amazon.com

CPSIA information can be obtained
at www.ICGtesting.com
Printed in the USA
LVHW112040110219
607156LV00001BA/41/P